LIFE SKILLS 2

GRATITUDE TO ALLAH SERIES

MONEY MANAGEMENT & EMPLOYMENT SKILLS

A Practical Guide for Muslims on Managing Work & Finances

FAITH
Publications

All thanks are due to Allah *subhaanahu wa ta'ala* for enabling us with this effort.
Special thanks to the following contributors:

Content Writer: Dr. Haroon Baqai
Editing Team: Amber Bokhari, Aisha Elahi, Abdul Qaadir Abdul Khaaliq, Dalia Elamawy, Sayeed Jaweed, Zara Tariq
Copy Editor: Amber Bokhari
Shari'ah Advisors: Sh. Sabri Benkahla & Safi Khan
Graphic and Layout Design: Farah Firman
Curriculum Coordinator: Samira Hingoro

A project of Dar-us-Salaam community, College Park, MD, USA
www.darussalaam.org

Copyright © 2023 FAITH Publications

All rights reserved.
No part of this publication may be reproduced, distributed, or transmitted in any form or by any means, including photocopying, recording, or other electronic or mechanical methods, without the prior written permission of the publisher, except in the case of brief quotations embodied in reviews and certain other noncommercial uses permitted by copyright law.

Printed in the United States of America

ISBN 979-8-9874006-1-6

For permission requests, write to the publisher at the address below.

FAITH Publications
5301 Edgewood Road
College Park, MD 20740, USA
Phone: 301-982-9848
email: iscurriculum@alhuda.org
faithpublications.org

TABLE OF CONTENTS

UNIT 1 | MONEY MANAGEMENT

CHAPTER	PG	
01	11	How Should You Manage Your Money?
02	21	How to Budget Effectively
03	29	How to Organize Your Finances
04	37	Ways to Increase Your Income & Debt Relief
05	45	What is Riba?
	50	Activity
06	55	The Importance of Contracts
	62	Activity
07	65	Business Transactions
	68	UNIT 1 Review & Reflect Questions

UNIT 2 | EMPLOYMENT SKILLS

CHAPTER	PG	
08	75	Getting Ready for a Career
	80	Activity
09	83	Working as a Muslim
	95	UNIT 2 Review & Reflect Questions
	96	Appendix

PREFACE

Living in an era of constant change, there is a desperate need for Muslims and especially for Muslim youth to navigate various aspects of life using authentic Islamic knowledge. It is through this knowledge that you will find stability in a chaotic world. This book, anchored in authentic Islamic knowledge, helps navigate life's murky waters and provides clarity and guidance for you as a Muslim youth.

"Money Management and Employment Skills" touches upon two important areas; managing money and acquiring and exhibiting a positive attitude at work.* As you embark on this journey of life, it is wise for you to learn about handling your personal finances and career according to the framework of Islam. Many are unaware of it. This lack of knowledge can be harmful for us in this world and affect us in the Hereafter.

It is equally important to know how to be a productive Muslim at work. From using an Allah-centric approach in choosing a career to maintaining healthy work habits and relationships at work, this book will equip you to start your life on the right footing, all the while keeping Allah the center of your every decision. Deriving the guidance from the Qur'an and the example of Prophet Muhammad *sallAllahu 'alayhi wa sallam*, this journey will transform the way you earn and spend your money.

This book is the second Life Skills book which is a part of our *Gratitude to Allah series*. This series belongs to a new Islamic Studies curriculum; a curriculum which aims to help you apply your faith to real world issues. It presents everyday, practical applications of Islam. We pray that this book helps you draw closer to Allah as you learn and apply the knowledge in this book to your daily life. Please send your feedback to iscurriculum@alhuda.org. We welcome any suggestions to improve this curriculum.

Lastly, we would like to thank Dr. Haroon Baqai for writing the units so beautifully and sharing with us his wealth of knowledge and experience. May Allah accept this effort from him and everyone who worked on this book, and more importantly, may Allah accept your efforts to draw closer to Him.

---

* In our future editions, we plan to add a third section on Zakaah.

UNIT 1
MONEY MANAGEMENT

UNIT 1
IMPORTANT VOCABULARY

AHADITH
Plural of *hadith*, sayings of the Prophet *sallAllahu 'alayhi wa sallam*

AR-RAQEEB
The All-Observing, a name of Allah

AYAAT
Verses of the Qur'an, plural form of Ayah (verse)

AYATUD-DAYN
Ayah in the Qur'an related to Debt

DEEN
Religion, the complete way of life worshipping Allah

DU'AA
Supplication

DUNYA
Worldly affairs or this world

HADITH QUDSI
The sayings of the Prophet *sallAllahu 'alayhi wa sallam* as revealed to him by Allah

HIKMAH
Wisdom

IMAN
Faith, belief, or conviction

MUEZZIN
The caller of the daily prayers

RABB
Lord, Sustainer, Cherisher, Master, refers to Allah

RIBA
Usury or interest

RIZQ
Provision. It includes everything that Allah has provided us with

SADAQAH
Defined as true or sincere. Being true to Allah. Refers to a voluntary deed or an act of kindness done sincerely for Allah.

SAHABAH
The companions of the Prophet *sallAllahu 'alayhi wa sallam*

SALAH
The obligatory five daily Islamic prayers

SUNNAH
The traditions and practices of the Prophet *sallAllahu 'alayhi wa sallam*

TAQWA
Fearing Allah and having consciousness of Him

UMMAH
Community of Muslims

TABLE OF CONTENTS

UNIT 1 | MONEY MANAGEMENT

CHAPTER	PG	
01	11	How Should You Manage Your Money?
02	21	How to Budget Effectively
03	29	How to Organize Your Finances
04	37	Ways to Increase Your Income & Debt Relief
05	45	What is Riba?
	50	Activity
06	55	Contracts
	62	Activity
07	65	Business Transactions
	68	UNIT 1 Review & Reflect Questions

ESSENTIAL QUESTIONS

This unit is designed to help answer the following questions.

1. How can money help you draw closer to Allah?

2. How does budgeting help develop our Islamic character?

3. How does the connection with Allah help increase our income?

4. How does *riba* impact our lives?

CHAPTER 1

How Should You Manage Your Money?

Islam is a complete way of life and is present in everything we do. It covers all aspects of our life from the cradle to the grave. Allah has provided us with guidance from the Qur'an and **Sunnah** to better ourselves and to make things easier upon us when we deal with different issues. Money management is an extremely important issue such that it is one of the five questions that we will be asked about on the Day of Judgment. The Prophet *sallAllahu 'alayhi wa sallam* informed us about it in the following *hadith*,

"The son of Adam will not be dismissed from his Lord on the Day of Resurrection until he is questioned about five matters: his life and how he lived it, his youth and how he expended it, **his wealth and how he earned it and he spent it**, *and how he acted upon his knowledge."* [1]

The importance of money management is also highlighted in one of the five pillars of Islam: Zakaah. Zakaah is a yearly 2.5% obligatory payment from those meeting a fixed minimum wealth requirement which is given for the benefit of society. Money collected for zakaah is given to certain groups of people as specified in the Qur'an. In this unit, we will discuss how money can be means of drawing closer to Allah, if used responsibly.

---

1. At-Tirmidhi

The reality is human beings love money and tend to do whatever they can to earn as much money as possible. Allah mentions about this love of money in the Qur'an,

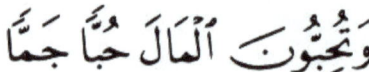

"And you love wealth with immense love." [2]

It is not bad to earn a lot of money as long as our approach to money and wealth is in line with the teachings of the Qur'an and the *Sunnah* of the Prophet *sallAllahu 'alayhi wa sallam*. Furthermore, we can enjoy our wealth, but we should never let it distract us from the main purpose of life; which is to worship Allah alone. Allah says in the Qur'an,

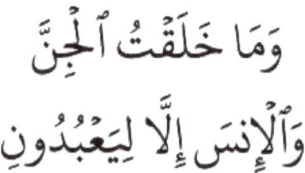

"And I did not create the jinn and mankind except to worship Me." [3]

Before we dive into the different aspects of building wealth, it is important that we consider a few important guiding principles, which will help us develop the right mindset.

PRINCIPLE #1

OBEDIENCE TO ALLAH AND HIS MESSENGER
sallAllahu 'alayhi wa sallam

Though the study of **iman** (belief) is not the subject of this book, it is very important to talk about as we learn about wealth management. *Iman* prompts us to obey Allah and His Messenger *sallAllahu 'alayhi wa sallam* in our daily interactions, which include money management and financial transactions. The qualities of trustworthiness, honesty and integrity are needed the most when managing money. It is our *iman* which guides us to these qualities and thus keeps us in obedience to Allah. Allah tells us in the Qur'an,

---

2. Surah Al-Fajr [89:20]
3. Surah Adh-Dhariyat [51:56]

Life Skills 2 Money Management & Employment Skills

OBEDIENCE IN ACTION

An orphan boy is trying to build a wall around his property, but the neighbor's tree is in the way. He asks the neighbor to give him that tree so he can build the wall around it. The neighbor refuses. The orphan complains to The Prophet and he, *sallAllahu 'alayhi wa sallam*, tells the neighbor that if he gives his tree to the orphan, then there would be a date palm tree for him in Jannah. The neighbor refuses. Abu Ad-Dahdah *radhiAllahu 'anhu* - the owner of one of the most famous orchards in Madinah is listening to this conversation. He asks The Prophet *sallAllahu 'alayhi wa sallam* that if he buys the tree from the neighbor and gives it to the orphan, would he get a date palm tree in Jannah? When The Prophet *sallAllahu 'alayhi wa sallam* responded yes, Abu Ad-Dahdah *radhiAllahu 'anhu* offered the neighbor his entire orchard to purchase the single tree. The neighbor agreed. The Prophet *sallAllahu 'alayhi wa sallam* repeatedly then says, "How many date palm trees (are there) in Jannah for Abu Ad-Dahdah!?" [6]

"*And whoever obeys Allah and the Messenger - they will be with those on whom Allah has bestowed His Grace and Favour from among the Prophets, the truthful who aided the truth, the martyrs and the righteous—how excellent these companions are!*" [4]

The Prophet *sallAllahu 'alayhi wa sallam* also informed us about the importance of our obedience to him as he said,

"*Everyone from my nation will enter Paradise but those who refuse.*" They said, "*O Messenger of Allah, who will refuse?*" The Prophet said, "*Whoever obeys me enters Paradise, and whoever disobeys me has refused.*" [5]

---

4. Surah An-Nisaa [4:69]
5. Sahih Al-Bukhari
6. Ahmad

PRINCIPLE #2

TAKE THE MIDDLE PATH

How do you strike the right balance between spending and saving? You may know of people who spend irresponsibly and then of others who won't even spend a cent. A unique characteristic of a Muslim is that they always try to take the middle path. A Muslim is not a spendthrift or a miser. As Allah tells us in the following *ayah*,

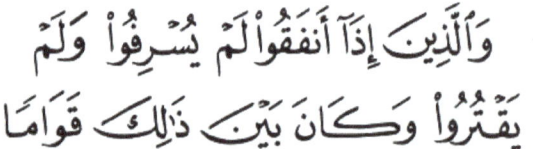

"And [they are] those who, when they spend, do so not excessively or sparingly but are ever, between that, [justly] moderate." [7]

In another *ayah*, Allah encourages us to avoid going to two extremes in being too stingy or too excessive. He tells us,

"And do not make your hand [as] chained to your neck or extend it completely and [thereby] become blamed and insolvent.[8]" [9]

PRINCIPLE #3

FOCUS ON THE HEREAFTER

Islam teaches us that whatever is in this world is temporary and that one day it will eventually come to an end. This is why focusing on the Hereafter is very important as that is where we will dwell forever. As believers, we know that money is something that we cannot take with us when we die. The Prophet *sallAllahu 'alayhi wa sallam* told us this in the following *hadith*,

"The dead person is followed by three: His family, his wealth and his deeds. Then two of them come back: His family and his wealth, and there remain only his deeds." [10]

---

7. Surah Al-Furqan [25:67]
8. Someone who is totally broke financially.
9. Surah Al-Israa' [17:29]
10. An-Nasa'ee

We know there is great importance in making money, but we have to remember to not let it consume or take us away from the remembrance of Allah and from the greater purpose of life, which is to attain the pleasure of Allah. Allah tells us in the Qur'an,

يَٰٓأَيُّهَا ٱلَّذِينَ ءَامَنُوا۟ لَا تُلْهِكُمْ أَمْوَٰلُكُمْ وَلَآ أَوْلَٰدُكُمْ عَن ذِكْرِ ٱللَّهِ ۚ وَمَن يَفْعَلْ ذَٰلِكَ فَأُو۟لَٰٓئِكَ هُمُ ٱلْخَٰسِرُونَ

"O you who have believed, let not your wealth and your children divert you from the remembrance of Allah. And whoever does that - then those are the losers." [11]

Thus, when we focus on the Hereafter and we don't make worldly affairs our greatest concern, it unshackles us from stress, tension and worries. It makes our hearts at peace. The Prophet *sallAllahu 'alayhi wa sallam* taught us the following *du'aa*,

وَلاَ تَجْعَلِ الدُّنْيَا أَكْبَرَ هَمِّنَا ، وَلاَ مَبْلَغَ عِلْمِنَا ، وَلاَ غَايَةَ رَغْبَتِنَا

"O Allah! let not worldly affairs (Dunya) be our principal concern (greatest aim), nor the ultimate limit of our knowledge nor the limit of our aspiration." [12]

---
11. Surah Al-Munafiqun [63:9]
12. At-Tirmidhi

As Muslims we should utilize whatever we have in this life to work hard for the Hereafter. And at the same time, we should not neglect what we have to earn in this world to live in it with ease. Allah tells us in the Qur'an,

وَٱبْتَغِ فِيمَآ ءَاتَىٰكَ ٱللَّهُ ٱلدَّارَ ٱلْءَاخِرَةَ وَلَا تَنسَ نَصِيبَكَ مِنَ ٱلدُّنْيَا

"But seek, through that which Allah has given you, the home of the Hereafter; and [yet], do not forget your share of the world." [13]

Focusing on the Hereafter does not mean that we do not utilize the necessary means to earn a living. We should earn a degree, get the necessary certifications that will enable us to get a decent job, strive for excellence in getting a job, and work hard in earning a good amount of money for our families and communities. As long as all these things do not consume us and do not take away our focus from our main purpose in life for which we were created, then there is no problem in seeking our share of this world.

---

13. Surah Al-Qasas [28:77]

🧠 BRAIN TEASER

Think of all the amazing things you own. Do you love your newest gadget that Allah has blessed you with? How can you use it to seek rewards in the Hereafter?

Love the car that your parents drive you in? If you had that car, how would you use it so that Allah is pleased with you?

As you earn money, buy a gadget, clothes, a car, a house, etc., compare these things to the Hereafter. Think, what would you need to earn or buy to improve your Hereafter?

IS BEING WEALTHY A BAD THING?

The simple answer to this question is no. There were several companions at the time of The Prophet *sallAllahu 'alayhi wa sallam* who were extremely wealthy, and were promised paradise. Of them were Abu Bakr As-Siddeeq and Abdurrahman Ibn 'Awf *radhiAllahu 'anhumaa*. They used their wealth to please Allah by spending on themselves, their families, and to support the cause of Islam. The Prophet *sallAllahu 'alayhi wa sallam* said about Abu Bakr *radhiAllahu 'anhu*,

"The wealth of no one has benefited me as much as the wealth of Abu Bakr." Abu Bakr wept and he said, *"My life and my wealth are only for you, O Messenger of Allah."* 14

If we keep the aforementioned principles in mind and utilize the wealth we are given in ways that please Allah, then our wealth can be a means for us to enter Jannah. But if we allow ourselves to be too busy accumulating wealth and spending that wealth only on ourselves, our wants and desires, then it could be a trial for us. Allah tells us in the Qur'an,

إِنَّمَآ أَمْوَٰلُكُمْ وَأَوْلَٰدُكُمْ فِتْنَةٌ وَٱللَّهُ عِندَهُۥٓ أَجْرٌ عَظِيمٌ

"Your wealth and your children are but a trial, and Allah has with Him a great reward." 15

In summary, there is nothing wrong with earning a lot of money as long as it does not take us away from the remembrance of Allah. If we utilize the money in a way that is pleasing to Allah (paying off someone's debt, donating to a masjid and Islamic school, help pay for someone's tuition in school or university, etc.) then it can even be a great blessing for us in both this world and the Hereafter. We must also understand that the money we have is provided to us by Allah to help us increase in goodness and humility and not a reason for anyone to become arrogant or prideful.

---

14. Ahmad
15. At-Taghabun [64:15]

DID YOU KNOW?

Allah tells us about a super rich person in the Qur'an called Qaarun. Who was Qaarun? Let us find out as Allah tells us:

"Indeed, Qaarun was from the people of Moses, but he tyrannized them. And We gave him of treasures whose keys would burden a band of strong men; thereupon his people said to him, "Do not exult. [16] Indeed, Allah does not like the exultant. But seek, through that which Allah has given you, the home of the Hereafter; and [yet], do not forget your share of the world. And do good as Allah has done good to you. And desire not corruption in the land. Indeed, Allah does not like corrupters.

He said, "I was only given it because of knowledge I have." Did he not know that Allah had destroyed before him of generations those who were greater than him in power and greater in accumulation [of wealth]? But the criminals, about their sins, will not be asked.

So he came out before his people in his adornment. Those who desired the worldly life said, Oh, would that we had like what was given to Qaarun. Indeed, he is one of great fortune.

But those who had been given knowledge said, "Woe to you! The reward of Allah is better for he who believes and does righteousness. And none are granted it except the patient.

And We caused the earth to swallow him and his home. And there was for him no company to aid him other than Allah, nor was he of those who [could] defend themselves.

And those who had wished for his position the previous day began to say, "Oh, how Allah extends provision to whom He wills of His servants and restricts it! If not that Allah had conferred favor on us, He would have caused it to swallow us. Oh, how the disbelievers do not succeed!

That home of the Hereafter We assign to those who do not desire exaltedness upon the earth or corruption. And the [best] outcome is for the righteous." [17]

POINTS TO PONDER

Can you think of any famous people today who make comments similar to Qaarun in which they attribute their hard work, intelligence, good fortune, and success to themselves? Do you find some people wanting to be like them just as some people wanted to be like Qaarun when they saw him flashing his wealth?

---

16. To express great pleasure or happiness; to rejoice exceedingly
17. Surah Al-Qasas [28: 76-84]

CHAPTER 2

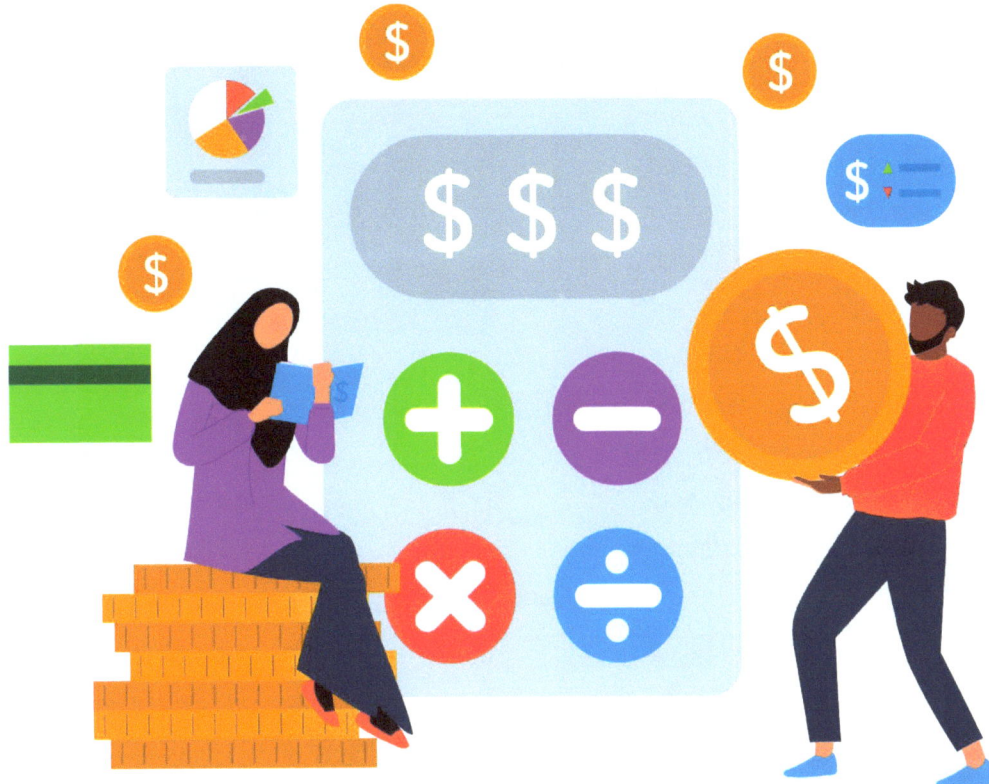

How To Budget Effectively

Budgeting is the process of creating a plan on how to spend your money. When you create a plan, it allows you to determine whether you have enough money to do the things you need to do and the things you would like to do. A budget is extremely important because without it, you may be wasting your money unknowingly and may find yourself running out of money before your next paycheck. Our wealth is limited and we must make the most use of it so we can live comfortably, benefit others with it, and spend towards our Hereafter. The best financial advice on budgeting has been shared with us by the Prophet *sallAllahu 'allayhi wa sallam* in the following *hadith*,

"While a man was walking through a barren land, he heard a voice coming out of a cloud, saying: 'Irrigate the garden of so-and-so.' Thereupon, the cloud drifted in a certain direction and discharged its water over a rocky plain. The streamlets flowed into a channel. This man followed the channel until it reached a garden and he saw the owner of the garden standing in its center, working with his spade to change the course of the water. He asked him: 'O slave of Allah,

what is your name?' He told his name, which was the same that he heard from the cloud. The owner of the garden then asked him: 'O slave of Allah, why did you ask my name?' He replied: 'I heard a voice from a cloud which poured down this water, saying: "Irrigate the garden of so-and-so." I would like to know what you do with it.' He said: 'Now that you asked me, I will tell you. I estimate the produce of the garden and distribute one-third of it in sadaqah, spend one-third on myself and my family, and invest one-third back into the garden.'" [18]

SADAQAH   FAMILY   FUTURE

Do you see how Allah provided for this man in ways he could not even imagine? When you start earning money, start off by dividing your earnings into these three categories; *sadaqah*, spending on your family, and investing for the future. Once you have completed the division, it is important to come up with sub-categories to see how you will budget yourself, so you do not end up spending too little or too much. Let us take a deeper dive into the three categories:

CATEGORY #1

GIVING SADAQAH

Living in a materialistic world, we are made to think that if you donate a part of your money, your money reduces by that amount. For example, if we have $2,000 in our account and we donate $500 from it, we will be left with $1,500. On the surface it may look as if our money has decreased, but the Prophet *sallAllahu 'alayhi wa sallam* told us in the following *hadith* that it does not:

> **SADAQAH DOES NOT DECREASE WEALTH.** [19]
>
> **Prophet Muhammad**
> *sallAllahu 'alayhi wa sallam*

---

18. Sahih Muslim
19. Sahih Muslim

Life Skills 2 Money Management & Employment Skills | 22

In the Qur'an, Allah equates the *sadaqah* we give to a loan that we are giving to Allah,

مَن ذَا ٱلَّذِى يُقْرِضُ ٱللَّهَ قَرْضًا حَسَنًا فَيُضَٰعِفَهُۥ لَهُۥ وَلَهُۥٓ أَجْرٌ كَرِيمٌ

"Who is it that would loan Allah a goodly loan so He will multiply it for him and he will have a noble reward?" [20]

BEST BUDGETING PRACTICES
PAYCHECK / MONEY

- SADAQAH — 1/3
- SELF & FAMILY — 1/3
- REINVEST — 1/3

In another *hadith* the the Prophet *sallAllahu 'alayhi wa sallam* tells us,

"Two angels descend every morning, and one says: 'O Allah, give him who spends something, in place of what he spends.' The other one says: 'O Allah, give destruction to him who withholds.'" [21]

As part of your budgeting process, an ideal start would be allocating one third of whatever you earn to give in the way of Allah. In fact, if you ever find yourself struggling financially and want to maximize your wealth, then giving in the way of Allah is the solution. Once The Prophet *sallAllahu 'alayhi wa sallam* was talking to Bilal *radhiAllahu 'anhu*, who was very poor. He, *sallAllahu 'alayhi wa sallam*, told Bilal [22] *radhiAllahu 'anhu*,

> SPEND IT, BILAL, AND DO NOT FEAR POVERTY FROM THE LORD OF THE THRONE. [23]

Prophet Muhammad
sallAllahu 'alayhi wa sallam

---

20. Surah Al-Hadid [57:11]
21. Sahih Al-Bukhari and Sahih Muslim
22. Famous, most trusted and loyal companion of the Prophet *sallAllahu 'alayhi wa sallam*. The first *muezzin* of Islam.
23. Al-Bayhaqi

FORGIVING LOANS

Giving someone a loan is a form of *sadaqah (being true to Allah)*. There is a special reward associated with giving someone a loan and then being lenient in asking for the repayment of the loan. The Prophet *sallAllahu 'alayhi wa sallam* said,

"Whoever gives respite to one in difficulty, he will have (the reward of) an act of charity for each day. Whoever gives him respite after payment becomes due, will have (the reward of) an act of charity equal to (the amount of the loan) for each day." [24]

As you prepare your budget, consider allocating a portion of your *sadaqah* money to help people with loans. It is a highly commendable act and very rewarding to lift a burden off of your fellow Muslim. The Prophet *sallAllahu 'alayhi wa sallam* said,

"A man would give loans to the people and he would say to his servant: If the debtor is in hardship you should forgive the debt so that perhaps Allah will relieve us. So when he met Allah, then Allah relieved him." [25]

CATEGORY #2

SPENDING ON YOUR FAMILY

Spending on your family includes paying for living expenses, utilities, food, clothes, and other necessities of life. Although a Muslim woman is free to work and even voluntarily help in taking care of her family financially, it is still the man's obligation to earn and spend on his family himself. Allah says in the Qur'an,

اَلرِّجَالُ قَوَّٰمُونَ عَلَى ٱلنِّسَآءِ بِمَا فَضَّلَ ٱللَّهُ بَعْضَهُمْ عَلَىٰ بَعْضٍ وَبِمَآ أَنفَقُوا۟ مِنْ أَمْوَٰلِهِمْ

"Men are in charge of women by [right of] what Allah has given one over the other and what they spend [for maintenance] from their wealth..." [26]

---

24. Ibn Majah
25. Sahih Al-Bukhari and Sahih Muslim
26. Surah An-Nisaa [4:34]

When spending on your family, we go back to the second principle mentioned earlier with regards to taking the middle path. This means that when you are spending on them, you should not be miserly or frugal in your spendings, and at the same time you should not overspend unnecessarily. There is a reward for those who spend on their family as mentioned by the Prophet *sallAllahu 'alayhi wa sallam*,

"When a Muslim spends something on his family intending to receive Allah's reward it is regarded as sadaqa for him." [27]

Budgeting can help a person plan out his or her expenses to make sure their family stays within their financial means. You can develop a budget by first listing all of the different expenses you and your family may have in a given month and then estimating how much each of those expenses may be.

DID YOU KNOW?

Some people think that it is disliked to buy nice and expensive things. They may purposefully have a shabby appearance and wear old clothes, thinking that that is Islamic. Then you may have some who look down upon those who buy fancy clothes, shoes, and or other things in life.

It was narrated from Abu Al-Ahwas, from his father, That he came to the Prophet *sallAllahu 'alayhi wa sallam* wearing shabby clothes. The Prophet *sallAllahu 'alayhi wa sallam* said to him: "Do you have any wealth?" He said: "Yes, all kinds of wealth." He said: "What kind of wealth?" He said: "Allah has given me camels, cattle, sheep, horses and slaves." He said: "If Allah has given you wealth, **then let the effect of Allah's blessing and generosity be seen on you.**" [28]

So remember, it's perfectly fine to buy nice things but don't let the latest trends and fashions cause you to buy excessively. Wealth can be enjoyed, but do not let it distract you. Always choose the middle path and be humble in your buying to avoid anything that will lead you to become arrogant or prideful.

---
27. Sahih Al-Bukhari
28. An-Nasa'ee

Some things you should include in your budget are:

1. RENT
2. UTILITIES
3. GROCERIES
4. CLOTHING
5. INSURANCE
6. GASOLINE
7. CAR EXPENSES

CATEGORY #3

INVESTING FOR THE FUTURE

Investing is a cost-effective way to put your money to work and potentially build more of your personal wealth. If you can find something **halal** *(lawful)* to invest in, then it would be ideal to invest one third, or a portion of your wealth into it. Before investing for the long-term, put aside at least six months worth of your monthly expenses for emergency purposes. For example, if your monthly expenses for your household is $4,000, then try to put aside $24,000 for emergency purposes. Having money set aside for your future is always the best and safest option.

HOW TO SAVE YOUR MONEY?

There are two types of bank accounts where one can save their money for emergency purposes:

1. CHECKING ACCOUNT

Most banks offer checking accounts, which allow you to deposit and withdraw money. Most banks also offer a check (or debit) card, which allows you to swipe your check card at a store, which directly withdraws money from your account. When opening your bank account, always open a non-interest bearing checking account. This means that the bank does not pay you any interest on the amount of money you have deposited in your account.

BEWARE and only swipe your check card/debit card when you know for certain that you have enough money in your account. If you swipe your check card but you do not have enough money in your account, then you may be charged an extra fee, some of which may also be considered *riba* (usury/interest).

HOW TO INVEST?

You can invest your money in any business that offers *halal* (islamically compliant) products and services, and finances its operations through *halal*, interest-free means. Some examples of investments may include:

> 1. Precious metals like gold and silver.
>
> 2. Companies that sell *halal* products and services.
>
> 3. Mutual funds or stocks, where the companies only sell *halal* products and services, and do not engage in any interest-bearing transactions.
>
> 4. Real estate; Buying a house with a non-interest loan or cash and renting it out to someone.

2 SAVINGS ACCOUNT

Most banks offer savings accounts, and encourage you to have one. Most of these savings accounts offer a small percentage of *riba* (usury/interest), which is prohibited for Muslims. As such, avoid opening any savings accounts.

We will discuss *riba* in more detail later in this unit.

Life Skills 2 *Money Management & Employment Skills* | 27

CHAPTER 3

How To Organize Your Finances

Organizing your finances will not only help you secure your future but it will also improve your day-to-day spending habits for the better. If you stay organized, you'll know the amount of money you'll have to spend each month and are less likely to get behind on bills. The issue of being organized is extremely important in Islam; it comes from the act of placing things where they belong - which is called **hikmah** (wisdom). You need to develop a clear and well-laid out system to organize your finances so you have an idea of how much money you have to spend, where you want to spend it and where you are currently spending it. There are many budgeting software tools available on the internet that can be used to develop and track a budget. Whichever one you choose, strive to be consistent and disciplined in implementing and following your budget. Once you have created a budget, you must stick to it!

A sample budgeting sheet is provided, which can be used as a starting point in developing your own budget.

MONTHLY BUDGET Planner

ITEMS	AMOUNT	NOTES
DIVIDE THE BI-WEEKLY AMOUNT BY THREE		
EXPENSES		
TAXES		
CAR		
RENT		
WATER		
GAS		
ELECTRICITY		
INTERNET		
PHONE		
GROCERIES		
CLOTHING		
SADAQAH		
FAMILY MEMBERS		
CLOSE RELATIVES		
MASJID		
ISLAMIC SCHOOL		
ORPHANS		
GIFTS		
LOANS		
INVESTMENTS		
PRECIOUS METALS		
MUTUAL FUNDS / STOCKS		
OTHER		
TOTAL		

MANAGING & PAYING BILLS

With the advancement of technology, it has now become easier to manage the different bills you have to pay. You may opt to receive paper bills for many of your expenses; however, electronic bills (eBills) are now more popular and the preferred method for most people.

When you are buying a product or service, you are essentially committing to pay for that product or service in a timely manner, which is a condition of purchase. Regardless of how you choose to manage and pay your bills, always make sure that you pay your bills on time. The Prophet *sallAllahu 'alayhi wa sallam* advised us in the following *hadith*,

> **THE MUSLIMS ARE BOUND BY THEIR CONDITIONS...** [29]
>
> **Prophet Muhammad**
> *sallAllahu 'alayhi wa sallam*

If you opt to receive and pay bills on paper (ex. using a check), then develop a system where you pay all your bills each month on time, or before their due date, and always steer clear of paying any bills late as late fees are considered interest and must be avoided.

If you opt for eBills, then:

1. Consider an auto-pay set up where the bills are automatically paid from your account before the due date.

2. Ensure that there is enough money in your bank account to automatically pay those bills.

---

29. At-Tirmidhi

Life Skills 2 Money Management & Employment Skills | 31

KHALID'S DILEMMA

Let us meet Khalid and see how his perception of a successful lifestyle is shaped by family, friends, and society. As you read through it, focus on what Khalid's thought process might be.

Khalid wants to go to college and graduate with a prestigious degree like the rest of his family, but he can't afford the college tuition. Instead of looking for *halal* options (grants, scholarships, work and save for college, etc) he takes on a $50,000 college loan, which he has to repay in 10 years, along with the interest. He knows that such interest-bearing loans are prohibited in Islam as he just heard a *khutbah* about it and so is very hesitant to do it. He finally convinces himself that a college degree is important and in order to get a good job and support himself and his family, it is a necessity.

Fast forward ten years. Khalid has now earned his degree and has a really good job. He now plans on paying his college loan back. Khalid and his college buddies get together weekly to hang out. When Khalid drives to one of these hangouts, he feels embarrassed parking his 15-year old Toyota Corolla next to his friends' brand new, shiny BMW, Lexus, or Mercedes. He does not have the cash to buy that kind of car; he cannot afford it. He takes a car loan and buys a brand new BMW with a $499 monthly payment. He justifies this decision by thinking that he **needs** a reliable car to get to work, which helps him earn his living.

A few months later, Khalid learns from listening to a personal financial planning webinar that a key to gaining financial independence is to own a house. Houses in Khalid's area cost no less than $400,000, which he does not have. All of his family members, uncles, and aunts, own large houses. How can he not buy one, even if it's a small one? He starts researching and finds a house that he likes. He takes a loan from the bank with a monthly mortgage of $2,100. His conscience pricks him a little; but he justifies what he is doing by thinking that he **needs** to have a house in order to be financially independent and stable.

On a monthly basis, Khalid now has to pay a monthly payment of his college loan, his brand new car, and his house mortgage. Most of the cash he receives from his salary goes toward paying these monthly payments. He can hardly maintain a regular cash flow for himself, let alone being able to pay any *sadaqah*. But he still hangs out with his friends, who all wear nice clothes, drive nice cars, have expensive watches, and maintain at least a twice-a-week eating out schedule. For Khalid, it becomes a convincing that he **needs** to buy all of those things to be happy. But he does not have the cash to afford all of this.

What does he do? He just received a special credit card offer in the mail, which offered a **free** credit card, and 1.5% cashback on all purchases. Meaning, that for every dollar that Khalid spends using his credit card, he earns 1.5 cents back; for every $100, he gets $1.5 cashback; for every $1,000, he gets $15 cash back. He jumps on the opportunity and gets the credit card. He starts paying for all of these expenses, like buying branded clothes, expensive shoes, fancy cars, and eats out with his friends at least twice a week. He does this all because he **needs** to hang out with friends for his mental peace and unwind after a busy work week; and he **needs** to wear nice clothes and drive nice cars so he is not an outcast.

When the time comes to pay for his credit card bill, he is unable to do it simply because he does not have the cash to pay for it. The credit card gives the opportunity to make a "minimum payment" on the bill (which is usually 1% - 3% of the total bill, including interest and late fees). He makes those payments and lets his credit card debt accumulate, which requires him to pay more interest.

Fast forward another ten years. Though Khalid has now been promoted and earns a high salary, he is still fully entangled in debt; paying interest on a monthly basis. He feels miserable and under so much pressure. He is under constant stress because of the numerous notices he gets from collection agencies trying to collect his unpaid debts. Though he has a good job, lives in a decent house and drives a nice car, he finds himself having to take sleeping pills to go to sleep because of all these pressures.

Khalid's situation is not a unique one. Many, if not most of the youth, go through this life cycle. Here are a few key issues that we can identify in these situations. Can you think of more?

1 SUCCESS IS HOW IT IS SHAPED IN OUR MINDS

For Khalid, and many people, success is often defined in material terms. Their frame of reference is based on the current trends in the society, which are constantly changing. For believers, the frame of reference is constant and most importantly follows the teachings of the Qur'an and *Sunnah*.

2 NORMALIZING INTEREST-BEARING ACTIVITIES

Because success is defined in material terms, people normalize the sin of interest, to the point that engaging in interest doesn't seem a big deal to them.

3 JUSTIFYING ACTIONS

As mentioned in the first two points, Khalid, like most people, made excuses and gave himself all the reasons to justify his actions and lifestyle.

4 MATERIAL THINGS PROVIDE TEMPORARY HAPPINESS

Khalid aspired for all these material things in pursuit of happiness. He did get happiness, but it was temporary because he spent his whole life owing money. On the other hand, there are people who do not have nearly as much as Khalid, but their lives are much more peaceful because they base their happiness on living the eternal life in the Hereafter.

Being a Muslim Employer

If you own a business and have employees or you hired someone to do work around the house, you must make sure you pay them on time. If you sign a contract or agree verbally with an employee or a temporary help about the amount of compensation and the time of payment, then it is crucial that you abide by your contract or agreement with them and pay them on time according to the agreement. The Prophet *sallAllahu 'alayhi wa sallam* told us in a **Hadith Qudsi.** [30]

"Allah, the Exalted, says: 'I will contend on the Day of Resurrection against three (types of) people: One who makes a covenant in My Name and then breaks it; one who sells a free man as a slave and devours his price; and one who hires a workman and having taken full work from him, does not pay him his wages." [31]

Respecting Laws

It does not matter what country you live in, you must remember to always abide by the laws of the land as long as they do not go against the Qur'an and the *Sunnah*. Allah tells us in the Qur'an,

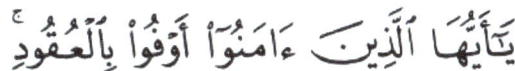

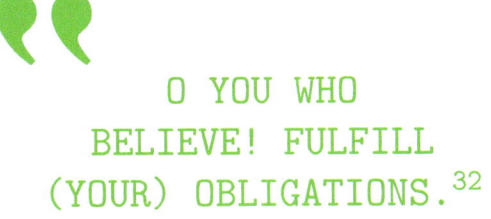

O YOU WHO BELIEVE! FULFILL (YOUR) OBLIGATIONS. [32]

Surah Al-Ma'idah

Every Muslim is obliged to follow the various laws of the land, such as paying taxes, paying for car insurance, paying for housing, paying for utilities, etc., and to do so with honesty and integrity. The Prophet *sallAllahu 'alayhi wa sallam* advised us,

"Give back what has been entrusted (to you) to him who has entrusted you, and do not violate the trust of him who violates your trust." [33]

The Prophet *sallAllahu 'alayhi wa sallam* also informed us in the following *hadith*, *"The signs of a hypocrite are three: Whenever he speaks, he tells a lie; and whenever he promises, he breaks his promise; and whenever he is entrusted, he betrays (proves to be dishonest)."* [34]

These *ahadith* emphasize the importance of taking care of our obligations.

---

30. *Hadith Quds*i is a special category of where the meaning is from Allah and the words are from the Prophet Muhammad *sallAllahu 'alayhi wa sallam*.
31. Sahih Al-Bukhari
32. Surah Al-Ma'idah [5:1]
33. Abu Dawood
34. Sahih Al-Bukhari and Sahih Muslim

CHAPTER 4

WAYS TO INCREASE YOUR INCOME & DEBT RELIEF

We find in the Qur'an and the *Sunnah* that Muslims are highly encouraged to seek out ways to increase their wealth. Allah tells us in the Qur'an,

*"And when the prayer has been concluded, disperse within the land and **seek from the bounty of Allah**, and remember Allah often that you may succeed."* [35]

Before we start to find ways of increasing our income, we must begin with being thankful to Allah and acknowledging the *rizq* (provision) and other blessings we already have in our lives. Allah says in the Qur'an,

وَإِذْ تَأَذَّنَ رَبُّكُمْ لَئِن شَكَرْتُمْ لَأَزِيدَنَّكُمْ

"And [remember] when your Lord proclaimed, 'If you are grateful, I will surely increase you [in favor]..." [36]

---

35. Surah Al-Jumu'ah [62:10]
36. Surah Ibrahim [14:7]

Life Skills 2 Money Management & Employment Skills | 37

Rizq is not limited to our wealth, but covers a vast number of areas like our talent, time, relationships, the love we have for each other, the sense of peace and tranquility that we may feel, and so on and so forth. Out of His ultimate wisdom and mercy, Allah has taught us many different ways to increase our *rizq*. Consider some of the following ways below:

HOW TO INCREASE YOUR *RIZQ*
ASK ALLAH FOR FORGIVENESS

EVIDENCE FROM THE QUR'AN AND SUNNAH

فَقُلْتُ اسْتَغْفِرُوا رَبَّكُمْ إِنَّهُ كَانَ غَفَّارًا
يُرْسِلِ السَّمَاءَ عَلَيْكُم مِّدْرَارًا

"And said, 'Ask forgiveness of your Lord. Indeed, He is Ever-Forgiving. He will send [rain from] the sky upon you in [continuing] showers." [37]

It was narrated from 'Abdullah bin 'Abbas that the Messenger of Allah *sallAllahu 'alayhi wa sallam* said: "Whoever persists in asking for forgiveness, Allah will grant him relief from every worry, and a way out from every hardship, and will grant him provision from (sources) he could never imagine." [38]

On the other hand, a person may be deprived of a form of *rizq* because of a sin that he or she may commit. The Prophet *sallAllahu 'alayhi wa sallam* told us,

"A man is deprived of provision because of the sins that he commits." [39]

---

37. Surah Nuh [71:10-11]
38. Ibn Majah
39. Ibn Majah

Life Skills 2 Money Management & Employment Skills | 38

HOW TO INCREASE YOUR *RIZQ*
BE DUTIFUL TO ALLAH AND HAVE TAQWA (FEAR OF ALLAH)

EVIDENCE FROM THE QUR'AN AND SUNNAH

وَمَن يَتَّقِ اللَّهَ يَجْعَل لَّهُ مَخْرَجًا وَيَرْزُقْهُ مِنْ حَيْثُ لَا يَحْتَسِبُ

"And whoever fears Allah - He will make for him a way out. And will provide for him from where he does not expect." [40]

Abu Dharr narrates that the Prophet *sallAllahu 'alayhi wa sallam* began to recite this *ayah* to me: *"And whoever fears Allah, He will find a way out for him"*, until he finished reciting it. Then he said, "O Abu Dharr, if the people were to take it (in the right spirit) it would suffice them." [41]

In another *ayah* Allah tells us,

وَلَوْ أَنَّ أَهْلَ الْقُرَىٰ آمَنُوا وَاتَّقَوْا لَفَتَحْنَا عَلَيْهِم بَرَكَاتٍ مِّنَ السَّمَاءِ وَالْأَرْضِ وَلَٰكِن كَذَّبُوا فَأَخَذْنَاهُم بِمَا كَانُوا يَكْسِبُونَ

"And if only the people of the cities had believed and feared Allah, We would have opened upon them blessings from heaven and the earth; but they denied [the messengers], so We seized them for what they were earning." [42]

---

40. Surah At-Talaaq [65:3]
41. Ahmad
42. Surah Al-'Araf [7:96]

HOW TO INCREASE YOUR *RIZQ*
FOCUS ON ALLAH AND THE HEREAFTER

EVIDENCE FROM THE QUR'AN AND SUNNAH

Abu Huraira *radhiAllahu 'anhu* reported: The Messenger of Allah *sallAllahu 'alayhi wa sallam* said: Allah said: "O son of Adam, be free for My worship and I will fill your heart with riches and alleviate your poverty. If you do not do so, I will fill your hands with problems and never alleviate your poverty." [43]

Zayd ibn Thabit *radhiAllahu 'anhu* reported: The Messenger of Allah *sallAllahu 'alayhi wa sallam* said, "Whoever is concerned about the world, Allah will disorder his affairs, make poverty appear before his eyes, he will not get anything from the world but what has been decreed for him. Whoever is concerned about the Hereafter, Allah will settle his affairs, make him content in his heart, the world will inevitably come to him." [44]

HOW TO INCREASE YOUR *RIZQ*
PERFORM HAJJ AND 'UMRAH

EVIDENCE FROM THE QUR'AN AND SUNNAH

Abdullah ibn Mas'ud *radhiAllahu 'anhu* reported: The Messenger of Allah *sallAllahu 'alayhi wa sallam* said, "Perform the Hajj and 'Umrah pilgrimages, one after another, for they both erase poverty and sins just as the furnace removes impurity from iron, gold, and silver. There is no reward for an accepted Hajj but Paradise." [45]

---

43. At-Tirmidhi
44. Ibn Majah
45. At-Tirmidhi

HOW TO INCREASE YOUR *RIZQ*
MAINTAIN RELATIONSHIP WITH RELATIVES

EVIDENCE FROM THE QUR'AN AND SUNNAH

Anas ibn Malik *radhiAllahu 'anhu* reported: The Messenger of Allah *sallAllahu 'alayhi wa sallam* said, "Whoever is pleased to have his provision expanded and his life span extended, let him keep good relations with his family." [46]

Ibn 'Umar *radhiAllahu 'anhu* said, "If someone fears his Lord and maintains ties of kinship, his term of life will be prolonged, he will have abundant wealth and his people will love him." [47]

HOW TO INCREASE YOUR *RIZQ*
SPEND IN THE WAY OF ALLAH

EVIDENCE FROM THE QUR'AN AND SUNNAH

Abu Huraira *radhiAllahu 'anhu* reported: The Messenger of Allah *sallAllahu 'alayhi wa sallam* said, "Allah said: Spend in *sadaqah*, O son of Adam, and I will spend on you." [48]

Abu Huraira *radhiAllahu 'anhu* reported: The Prophet *sallAllahu 'alayhi wa sallam* said, "Two angels descend every morning, and one says: 'O Allah, give him who spends something, in place of what he spends.' The other one says: 'O Allah, give destruction to him who withholds.'" [49]

---

46. Sahih Al-Bukhari and Sahih Muslim
47. Sahih Al-Bukhari
48. Sahih Al-Bukhari and Sahih Muslim
49. Sahih Al-Bukhari and Sahih Muslim

HOW TO INCREASE YOUR *RIZQ*
SPEND ON STUDENTS

EVIDENCE FROM THE QUR'AN AND SUNNAH

Anas ibn Malik *radhiAllahu 'anhu* reported: There were two brothers during the time of the Prophet *sallAllahu 'alayhi wa sallam*. One of them used to come to the Prophet *sallAllahu 'alayhi wa sallam* (frequently attend the lessons of the Prophet *sallAllahu 'alayhi wa sallam*) and the other used to work to earn a living. Once, the working brother complained to the Prophet *sallAllahu 'alayhi wa sallam* about his brother. Thereupon, he replied: "Perhaps you are granted sustenance because of him." [50]

HOW TO INCREASE YOUR *RIZQ*
FOLLOW THE QUR'AN AND SUNNAH

EVIDENCE FROM THE QUR'AN AND SUNNAH

وَلَوْ أَنَّهُمْ أَقَامُوا التَّوْرَاةَ وَالْإِنجِيلَ وَمَا أُنزِلَ إِلَيْهِم مِّن رَّبِّهِمْ لَأَكَلُوا مِن فَوْقِهِمْ وَمِن تَحْتِ أَرْجُلِهِم ۚ مِّنْهُمْ أُمَّةٌ مُّقْتَصِدَةٌ ۖ وَكَثِيرٌ مِّنْهُمْ سَاءَ مَا يَعْمَلُونَ

"And if only they upheld [the law of] the Torah, the Gospel (as it was revealed in its original form) and what has been revealed to them from their Lord, they would have consumed [provision] from above them and from beneath their feet. Among them are a moderate community, but many of them - evil is that which they do." [51]

---

50. At-Tirmidhi
51. Surah Al-Ma'idah [5:66]

HOW TO INCREASE YOUR RIZQ
STARTING THE DAY EARLY

EVIDENCE FROM THE QUR'AN AND SUNNAH

اللَّهُمَّ بَارِكْ لِأُمَّتِي فِي بُكُورِهَا

The Prophet *sallAllahu 'alayhi wa sallam* said: "O Allah, bless my people in their early mornings." When he sent out a detachment or an army, he sent them at the beginning of the day. Sakhr was a merchant, and he would send off his merchandise at the beginning of the day; and he became rich and had much wealth." [52]

---

52. Abu Dawood

CHAPTER 5

WHAT IS RIBA?

Riba is an Arabic word which means "to increase" or "to exceed" and it is commonly translated to mean 'usury' or 'interest'. *Riba* is money paid at a particular rate of increase over time for the use of money that was borrowed, or for delay in repaying a debt beyond a loan or a debt's specified life. Allah tells us in the Qur'an,

يَٰٓأَيُّهَا ٱلَّذِينَ ءَامَنُوا۟ لَا تَأْكُلُوا۟ ٱلرِّبَوٰٓا۟ أَضْعَٰفًا مُّضَٰعَفَةً وَٱتَّقُوا۟ ٱللَّهَ لَعَلَّكُمْ تُفْلِحُونَ

"O you who have believed, **do not consume usury**, doubled and multiplied, but fear Allah that you may be successful." [53]

---

53. Surah Ale-'Imran [3:130]

THE PROHIBITION OF RIBA

There can be many discussions on why *riba* is prohibited in Islam. Such as 'it makes the poor poorer and the rich richer.' However, the first and foremost reason why we as Muslims are obliged to stay away from it is because it is an order from Allah. Allah tells us in the Qur'an,

ٱلَّذِينَ يَأْكُلُونَ ٱلرِّبَوٰا۟ لَا يَقُومُونَ إِلَّا كَمَا يَقُومُ ٱلَّذِى يَتَخَبَّطُهُ ٱلشَّيْطَٰنُ مِنَ ٱلْمَسِّ ذَٰلِكَ بِأَنَّهُمْ قَالُوٓا۟ إِنَّمَا ٱلْبَيْعُ مِثْلُ ٱلرِّبَوٰا۟ وَأَحَلَّ ٱللَّهُ ٱلْبَيْعَ وَحَرَّمَ ٱلرِّبَوٰا۟ فَمَن جَآءَهُۥ مَوْعِظَةٌ مِّن رَّبِّهِۦ فَٱنتَهَىٰ فَلَهُۥ مَا سَلَفَ وَأَمْرُهُۥٓ إِلَى ٱللَّهِ وَمَنْ عَادَ فَأُو۟لَٰٓئِكَ أَصْحَٰبُ ٱلنَّارِ هُمْ فِيهَا خَٰلِدُونَ

يَمْحَقُ ٱللَّهُ ٱلرِّبَوٰا۟ وَيُرْبِى ٱلصَّدَقَٰتِ وَٱللَّهُ لَا يُحِبُّ كُلَّ كَفَّارٍ أَثِيمٍ

Those who consume interest cannot stand [on the Day of Resurrection] except as one stands who is being beaten by Satan into insanity. That is because they say, "Trade is [just] like interest." But Allah has permitted trade and has forbidden interest. So whoever has received an admonition from his Lord and desists may have what is past, and his affair rests with Allah. But whoever returns to [dealing in interest or usury] - those are the companions of the Fire; they will abide eternally therein. Allah destroys interest and gives increase for charities. And Allah does not like every sinning disbeliever. [54]

An example of interest is when a person borrows money and is unable to pay at a specified time, he then is charged an additional fee and by the time his debt is paid off, he would have paid much more than the original amount he borrowed. This causes hardship on the borrower and strains him financially. In another *ayah*,

Allah emphasizes to us the danger of *riba* by declaring a war against those who engage in it. Most people feel afraid to fight someone who is much bigger and stronger than them. Imagine being at war with Allah. Could anything in this world be worth waging a war with your Creator?

Allah says,

يَٰٓأَيُّهَا ٱلَّذِينَ ءَامَنُوا۟ ٱتَّقُوا۟ ٱللَّهَ وَذَرُوا۟ مَا بَقِىَ مِنَ ٱلرِّبَوٰٓا۟ إِن كُنتُم مُّؤْمِنِينَ فَإِن لَّمْ تَفْعَلُوا۟ فَأْذَنُوا۟ بِحَرْبٍ مِّنَ ٱللَّهِ وَرَسُولِهِۦ ۖ وَإِن تُبْتُمْ فَلَكُمْ رُءُوسُ أَمْوَٰلِكُمْ لَا تَظْلِمُونَ وَلَا تُظْلَمُونَ

"O you who have believed, fear Allah and give up what remains [due to you] of interest, if you should be believers. And if you do not, then be informed of a war [against you] from Allah and His Messenger. But if you repent, you may have your principal - [thus] you do no wrong, nor are you wronged." [55]

---

54. Surah Al-Baqarah [2:275-276]
55. Surah Al-Baqarah [2:278-279]

🧠 BRAIN TEASER

As you gear up to enter college and the post-college world, consider your frame of mind. How do you define success? How is happiness sought? How often do you find yourself justifying your actions, versus acknowledging your shortcomings and sincerely committing to improve?

The Prophet *sallAllahu 'alayhi wa sallam* warned us to avoid the seven destructive sins. *Riba* is one of them. He said,

"Avoid the seven destructive things." It was asked: (by those present): "What are they, O Messenger of Allah?" He replied, "Associating partners with Allah; magic; killing an innocent person except by legal right; consuming usury; consuming the property of an orphan; retreating from the battlefield; slandering chaste, innocent and believing women." [56]

The severity of *riba* is not limited to the person who is involved in the *riba*, but rather anyone who directly participates in it as well. It was narrated in the following *hadith*,

"Allah's Messenger cursed the one who accepted usury, the one who paid it, the one who recorded it, and the two witnesses to it, saying they were all alike." [57]

Sadly, society today heavily encourages *riba* and its consumption. It's a difficult time to live in when we know the world runs on it. But in order for us to be successful in this world and the Hereafter, we must prioritize our obedience to Allah and His messenger *sallAllahu 'alayhi wa sallam* and completely stay away from it.

---

56. Sahih Al-Bukhari and Sahih Muslim
57. Sahih Muslim

THIS IS RIBA

Asiya takes on a college loan paying $200 per month. For every month she borrows, the finance company is asking her to pay back $225 in return. This extra $25 each month is interest (riba).

She should not have to pay extra money when borrowing money. In Islam, what is required is that she pays back exactly what she borrowed and no additions should be added.

Always remember... If you are taking a college loan, car loan or any type of loan make sure you are only repaying exactly what you paid and no additions!

ACTIVITY

Consider the following scenarios and how would you respond to each of them?

1. AMINAH, AND HER CREDIT CARD BILL

Aminah lives in the United States. She has a credit card bill of $3,300 but she does not have that money in her account. She tells you that she does not plan on paying the $3,300 because at the end of the day, she is dealing with a rich bank.

2. ZAYD, THE CLEVER BUSINESSMAN

Zayd owns a gas station with an attached convenience store and an auto-repairing shop with two employees. At the end of each year, he has to report all of his sales for tax purposes. He also has to report how much he paid each employee so he can pay his portion of taxes on their salaries. He considers himself a smart businessman, so in order to save money, he does a few things:

1
For all the things he sells in his convenience store by cash, he does not report those sales to avoid paying sales tax. "No one from the government would ever know about those cash sales, anyways," he thinks to himself.

2
For his employees, he pays them using the cash he gets from his sales. That way he does not have to pay taxes on their salaries, and they will not have to pay any income tax either.

3
Zayd thinks that this is a form of clever business, where he will be earning more money. And after all, the tax money would have gone to the non-Muslims anyway.

3. AHMAD, THE MECHANIC WHO WORKS FOR ZAYD

Ahmad is a mechanic who works for Zayd. He earns $5,000 in cash every month, all of which is not reported. He does not pay any tax on it. In addition, he has a low-income housing program in his local county, where the county covers most of the rental cost. He also reports to his county that he hardly earned any money and as such, gets most of his rent covered through the county as well. Additionally, he participates in the local food stamps program, which is specifically for those people who do not have enough income to provide food on their table.

4. ADAM, THE RICH LENDER

Adam is a rich man, and the loyal friend that lends money. Adam has been helping his friends out financially whenever they need it. Most recently, he lent $2000 to his friend Tariq to help him pay off his rent and he told Tariq he can pay it all off in five months for $2500. Adam feels since he is helping people out there is no harm in making profit off of them.

5. Yasmine's & Ahmad's Budget

The chart below shows how much Yasmine and Ahmad spent and saved with their February pay. If each of them continues to spend and save similarly in March and April, what do you think will happen by the end of April for both of them?

Yasmine's expenses and savings for FEBRUARY

EXPENSES	AMOUNT
FOOD	$700
TRANSPORTATION	$300
CLOTHES	$450
RENT	$1000
SAVINGS	$50

Ahmad's expenses and savings for FEBRUARY

EXPENSES	AMOUNT
FOOD	$500
TRANSPORTATION	$200 *walks a few times a week*
CLOTHES	$100
RENT	$800
SAVINGS	$200

6. Budgeting tips

Saleem always pays his bills on time but struggles every month to support his family financially. He is worried that if some big emergency expense comes up, he won't be able to handle it. What budgeting tips would be helpful for him to start doing to help relieve himself from that worry?

CHAPTER 6

CONTRACTS

On a daily basis, we engage in a multitude of contracts and in order to protect all parties from any types of injustice, Islam places great importance on doing them. Some contracts may be written and others may be verbal. Both are considered binding contracts. However, it is highly recommended to write them down to avoid any issues that may arise. As a believer, it is part of our faith to always fulfill those contracts to the best of our ability no matter how big or small they are. Allah tells us in the Qur'an,

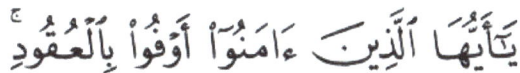

"O you who believe! Fulfill (your obligations)." [58]

The Prophet *sallAllahu 'alayhi wa sallam* told us that we must act upon the conditions we agree to. He mentions this in the following *hadith*,

---

58. Surah Al-Ma'idah [5:1]

*"The Muslims are **bound** by their conditions..."* [59]

Some common types of contracts that will be discussed in this chapter are:

> 1. **LOAN CONTRACTS**
>   - Car Loan
>   - House Loan
>   - College Loan
>   - Credit Card
> 2. **EMPLOYMENT CONTRACTS**

LOAN CONTRACTS

A **loan contract** is a written agreement between a lender that lends money to a borrower in exchange for repayment. In most cases, it involves interest. As we discussed earlier, if a loan involves interest, then it is completely prohibited. However, even if there is no interest involved, it is something one should be careful in getting into unless there is a real need to do so. Let's take a look at these important *hadith* to understand how loans affect not only us in this world but also in the Hereafter. The Prophet sallAllahu 'alayhi wa sallam said,

"Anyone whose soul leaves his body and he is free of three things, will enter Paradise: Arrogance, stealing from the spoils of war, and debt." [60]

The Prophet sallAllahu 'alayhi wa sallam told us,

"The soul of the believer is suspended because of his debt until it is paid off." [61]

In another *hadith* Prophet sallAllahu 'alayhi wa sallam said,

"By Him in whose hand Muhammad's soul is, if a man were to be killed in Allah's path then come to life, be killed again in Allah's path then come to life, and be killed once more in Allah's path then come to life owing a debt, he would not enter paradise till his debt was paid." [62]

The Prophet sallAllahu 'alayhi wa sallam tied our entrance to Jannah to our debt being repaid. Living in a "buy now pay later" society we should avoid getting in debt.

---

59. At-Tirmidhi
60. Ibn Majah
61. At-Tirmidhi
62. An-Nasa'ee

Life Skills 2 Money Management & Employment Skills

Handling Debt

If you find yourself in a financial situation where taking a loan is the only option, then make sure it is an interest free loan. It is important to work hard to pay it off or have a sincere intention to pay it off. In addition, your actions always must be coupled with *du'aa*. As Muslims, we understand that Allah only can remove our problems. Therefore, we must seek His help in every situation. The Prophet *sallAllahu 'alayhi wa sallam* used to make this *du'aa*,

اللَّهُمَّ إِنِّي أَعُوذُ بِكَ مِنَ الْهَمِّ وَالْحَزَنِ، وَالْعَجْزِ وَالْكَسَلِ، وَالْجُبْنِ وَالْبُخْلِ، وَضَلَعِ الدَّيْنِ، وَغَلَبَةِ الرِّجَالِ.

"O' Allah! I seek refuge with you from worry and sadness, from incapacity and laziness, from cowardice and miserliness, from being heavily in debt and from being overpowered by (other) men." [63]

---

63. Sahih Al-Bukhari

DID YOU KNOW?

Ayatud-dayn (Verse of Debt) is the longest *ayah* in the entire Qur'an taking up an entire page. The *ayah* goes into great details about debts, loans and loan contracts. There are many lessons, rules, and regulations that we learn from this one *ayah*. Allah says in the Qur'an,

"O you who have believed, when you contract a debt for a specified term, write it down. And let a scribe write [it] between you in justice. Let no scribe refuse to write as Allah has taught him. So let him write and let the one who has the obligation [i.e., the debtor] dictate. And let him fear Allah, his Lord, and not leave anything out of it. But if the one who has the obligation is of limited understanding or weak or unable to dictate himself, then let his guardian dictate in justice. And bring to witness two witnesses from among your men. And if there are not two men [available], then a man and two women from those whom you accept as witnesses - so that if one of them [i.e., the women] errs, then the other can remind her. And let not the witnesses refuse when they are called upon. And do not be [too] weary to write it, whether it is small or large, for its [specified] term. That is more just in the sight of Allah and stronger as evidence and more likely to prevent doubt between you, except when it is an immediate transaction which you conduct among yourselves. For [then] there is no blame upon you if you do not write it. And take witnesses when you conclude a contract. Let no scribe be harmed or any witness. For if you do so, indeed, it is [grave] disobedience in you. And fear Allah. And Allah teaches you. And Allah is Knowing of all things." [64]

---

64. Surah Al-Baqarah [2:282]

Common Types of Loan Contracts

Most people come across loan contracts when getting a college loan, car/auto loan, and or a house loan. College loans help students pay for college to cover educational expenses.

1. Car Loans

Car loans help those who cannot afford to buy a car. Most of the car loans are interest based except when a car manufacturer or dealership offers no interest financing on the car. Payment is usually done in installments. Interest based loans will include interest charges.

2. House loans

House loans are similar to car loans but usually take many many more years to pay back. In many countries, buying a house is not just considered a place to live but also an investment which is used to create wealth in the future. However, all non-Muslim based mortgages are interest based hence generally not allowed. In the absence of Muslim interest free financing options, you should continue to rent where you live instead of taking out an interest based mortgage. With all these loans, like we mentioned earlier, it would be permissible to take them only if there is no *riba* (interest) involved in them. Repayment of the loans must be equivalent to how much you initially paid.

3. College Loans

American Muslims Jur*ist*s in their recent ruling mentioned, *"It is permissible for a Muslim student to receive a subsidized loan if he believes that he will be able to repay all of it during the specific period. If he has a true need for such a loan."* For details see appendix in the back of the book.

4. Credit Card

A credit card contract is a type of loan. It is a contract to borrow money that will be paid back over time. There will be an extra charge (ex. *riba*) when paying back if the bill is not paid on time. The credit card company usually stipulates the amount of interest the cardholder will be charged if they did not pay their bill by the due date. This rate is called the Annual Percentage Rate (APR). By getting a credit card, you, by default, are signing a contract agreeing to pay that interest if you did not pay your bill on time. The Prophet *sallAllahu 'alayhi wa sallam* said,

"Allah's Messenger cursed the one who accepted usury, the one who paid it, the one who recorded it, and the two witnesses to it, saying they were all alike." [66]

Obtaining a credit card requires one to agree to terms and conditions, which include having to pay *riba*. Hence, in light of the *hadith* mentioned above, the ruling on getting credit cards is that it is not allowed. However, citing an Islamic maxim which says, *"necessities make forbidden things permissible,"* some scholars allow its usage in circumstances which mandates its use when there is no other solution. When using a credit card you have to make sure that the entire balance on the credit card should be paid in a specified time before interest is charged.

EMPLOYMENT CONTRACTS

Employers offer contracts to their employees, which outline the terms and conditions of their employment, compensation, and benefits that employees may receive while working. As Muslims, we should abide by the terms and conditions of the contract and always make sure to let our supervisors know if we are unable to fulfill some parts of the contract, so they can decide accordingly.

When you sign any contract to work, you must spend the minimum number of hours as detailed in your contract. Remember, if you are paid according to the number of hours that you work, then you must honestly record the number of hours you have actually worked. If you get paid for more hours than you have worked, then the income you are earning is not *halal*. The Prophet *sallAllahu 'alayhi wa sallam* advised us,

"Allah is good and accepts only what is good, and He has given the same command to the believers as He has given to the Messengers, saying, "O Messengers, eat of what is good and act righteously" [67] *and also, "You who believe, eat of the good things which We have provided for you."* [68] *Then he mentioned a man who makes a long journey in a disheveled and dusty state, who stretches out his hands to heaven saying,* **"My Lord, my Lord," when his food, drink and clothing are of an unlawful nature, and he is nourished by what is unlawful, and asked how such a one could be given an answer."** [69]

---

66. Sahih Muslim
67. Surah Al-Mu'minun [23:51]
68. Surah Al-Baqarah [2:172]
69. Sahih Muslim

DID YOU KNOW?

What should you do if you are done with all your assigned work at your job and now have free time? Consider the following:

- Inform your supervisor when you are finished with your work assignment and ask them if they would like to assign you something new.

- With your supervisor's permission, engage in some learning activity that would enhance your job skills and enable you to perform better at your job.

- If your supervisor or your workplace policy allows you to engage in personal tasks at work, then it should only be done as long as it doesn't affect your work. Examples of personal tasks may include, shopping online, updating your social media accounts, watching online videos, catching up on sports and business news, leaving work to run personal errands, etc.

ACTIVITY

There are some aspects of an employment contract that people tend to take lightly. Let us look at a few examples of how someone might violate part of their employment contract:

1

Jameel works very hard as an accountant. However, without the permission of his supervisor or a workplace policy which allows him to do personal work, he runs personal errands during his work hours, spends time browsing online, reads the news, watches sports highlights, and updates his social media accounts. He thinks it is normal because everyone else does it all the time.

2

Khadijah works at a school; every week she takes some of the stationery from her workplace to her home for personal use.

3

Hasan routinely comes to work late or leaves work early because he does not want to miss watching his favorite TV shows at home.

4

Ahmad works remotely from home. He has managed to get two full-time jobs, both of which require him to work eight hours a day. He logs in to both systems from home at the same time, making it seem as if he's completing his hours, but he really only spends a total of 10 hours on both jobs, combined.

Can you identify what is wrong in all of the above situations?

CHAPTER 7

BUSINESS TRANSACTIONS

We come across many business transactions on any given day - whether it is purchasing something in a store or online. These business transactions also have an inherent contract where the buyer is agreeing to buy the product or service at a given price, and the seller is agreeing to sell the product or service in an acceptable and known condition to the buyer. When conducting any business transactions, a general rule of thumb is given as explained in the following hadith of the Prophet sallAllahu 'alayhi wa sallam,

"The two parties to a transaction both have the choice so long as they have not separated, unless they have both chosen to conclude the transaction. If they have both chosen to conclude the transaction, then the transaction is binding." [70]

This means that if you are purchasing a product from someone, you have the right to cancel that business transaction as long as you have not left the person or the store. For example, if you are purchasing a shirt from a store, you have the right to cancel the transaction as long as you have not left the cashier. Once you have left the cashier, the sale is binding.

---

70. An-Nasa'ee

CAN WE RETURN SOMETHING WE PURCHASED?

As mentioned earlier the Prophet *sallAllahu 'alayhi wa sallam* told us,

"The Muslims are **bound** by their conditions..." [71]

If you purchase an item and the seller allows for it to be returned, then you may return it as long as the conditions of that return are fulfilled. For example, the seller may require that all returns must be within 30 days and items must be unused. In such a case, if you have used the item, then you may not return it even if the store employees do not know about it.

---

71. At-Tirmidhi

Consider these examples:

1 Salma has a few weddings to attend in the upcoming weeks. She goes to the store and buys a very expensive dress with the intention that she will return the dress after she wears the dress at the weddings. The store policy is that unused items can be returned with a receipt within 60 days. Salma wears the dress to the different weddings; after 50 days, she carefully cleans the dress, puts the tag back on, and returns it to the store to get a full refund. Do you think what Salma did was correct?

2 Fahad sees that a nearby store that offers a generous one-year return policy now carries one of the best vacuum cleaners in the market. He thinks of a bright idea to vacuum his house for free. He buys the vacuum, uses it in his house for 11 months, and then cleans it up, puts it back in its original packaging, and returns it to the store. Do you think what Fahad is doing is right?

In both of the examples, the buyer bought the item but his or her intention was to use the item and take advantage of the return policy. Remember the *hadith*,

"Actions are according to intentions..." [72]

Since their intentions were to take advantage of (or abuse) the return policy, their actions were incorrect. Even though the store employees may not have been able to catch their abuse. The Prophet *sallAllahu 'alayhi wa sallam* advised us,

> ...HE WHO DECEIVES IS NOT OF ME
> (IS NOT MY FOLLOWER) [73]
>
> **Prophet Muhammad**
> *sallAllahu 'alayhi wa sallam*

Deceiving is far from being a trait of a believer. Islam has stressed the importance of honesty in business transactions and in all matters. When a person is dishonest in his dealings, he must remember that Allah, **Ar-Raqeeb** (The All-Observing) is watching and he will be held accountable.

---
72. Sahih Al-Bukhari and Sahih Muslim
73. Sahih Muslim

▶ UNIT 1

REVIEW AND REFLECT QUESTIONS

1

Hisham has been saving his money for five years to build a home for him and his wife. Every time a fundraiser happens in the mosque he does not want to donate a single penny because he believes it will cause a loss towards his goal of building a home. How can you encourage Hisham to spend for the sake of Allah?

2

Maymuna is the only seventeen year old amongst her friends that has a job. After every Jumuah, Maymuna and her friends go out for pizza. Since none of her other friends work, Maymuna volunteers to pay for the pizza each week. Do you think Maymuna's spending habits are wise? How can her friends help Maymuna out?

Life Skills 2 Money Management & Employment Skills

3

Naeem was visiting his Uncle and could not help but notice that his Uncle's home was filled with expensive things. He had the latest coffee maker, an automatic vacuum cleaner, and a big chandelier in the dining room. He thought to himself that his Uncle seems to not value money and waste it on these useless things. What do you think about Naeem's perception of his Uncle and his fancy belongings?

4

Yunus wants to open an account at the bank. He goes to the bank and the sales clerk encourages him to open up a savings account. He is unsure, so he asks you which one is best for Muslims. What important points should you share with Yunus about saving accounts?

5

Make a comparison chart on how you would spend your allowance normally and how you would spend it if you had a budget.

6

Hassan got a job offer that will pay for not only the work he will do, but will also pay for his monthly rent and groceries. The only issue that comes up is that the company's main source of income is through *riba*. What should Hassan do and why?

UNIT 2
EMPLOYMENT SKILLS

UNIT 2

IMPORTANT VOCABULARY

AYAH
Verse from the Qur'an

DUNYA
This world

HADITH
A saying of the Prophet *sallAllahu 'alayhi wa sallam*

HALAL
Lawful or permissible

HARAM
Unlawful or prohibited

JANNAH
Paradise

MAHRAM
Referring to a husband, wife or a family member with whom marriage is not allowed

SALAAH
Prayer

SALAAT UL-JUMU'AH
Friday prayer

SAJDAH
Prostration

WUDHU
Ritual purification used for cleansing specific parts of the body

TABLE OF CONTENTS

UNIT 2 | EMPLOYMENT SKILLS

CHAPTER	PG	
08	75	Getting Ready for a Career
	80	Activity
09	83	Working as a Muslim
	95	UNIT 2 Review & Reflect Questions
	96	Appendix

ESSENTIAL QUESTIONS

This unit is designed to help answer the following questions.

1. "Islam is a way of life"- how does this affect us when choosing a career and in workplace behavior?

2. How can you use Islamic work ethic as a form of da'wah in the workplace?

3. Do matters such as *riba* and *haram* income impact our overall well-being?

4. How can we show tolerance and respect in the workplace without compromising our Islamic belief?

Life Skills 2 *Money Management & Employment Skills* | 73

CHAPTER 8

GETTING READY FOR A CAREER

Before we start thinking about what career we want to choose, as Muslims we must know the proper way to approach a career. Knowing this will help us achieve success in our careers as well as in the Hereafter.

1 BEING PRODUCTIVE

Every Muslim should make an effort to be a productive member of the society they live in. Hard work is one of the most important characteristics of a Muslim.

A person who works hard will see their efforts when providing for their family and others. The Prophet *sallAllahu 'alayhi wa sallam* said,

"By him in whose hand is my soul, if one of you were to carry a bundle of firewood on his back and sell it, that would be better for him than begging a man who may or may not give him anything." [74]

In another *hadith* the Prophet

---
74. Sahih Al-Bukhari

sallAllahu 'alayhi wa sallam said,

"Nobody has ever eaten a better meal than that which one has earned by working with one's own hands." [75]

2 EARNING HALAL INCOME

Our efforts to work and make sure we earn a *halal income* [76] is also very important as it affects our relationship with Allah. If our income is not *halal* then our *du'aas* will not be accepted.

3 WHAT IS HALAL INCOME?

There must be an effort made to make sure our income is from sources which are considered Islamically lawful and not from unlawful sources (such as, selling alcohol, lottery tickets, monetizing from social media content which is lewd, vulgar, dishonoring people, spreading fake information and anything which is displeasing to Allah, etc).

---

75. Sahih Al-Bukhari
76. Income which is considered lawful in Islamic shari'ah.

AVOID THESE CAREERS

When choosing a job or a career avoid working for a company that is involved in selling prohibited products or services. Here are some examples of places where we should avoid working at:

- A store that sells liquor, pork or lottery.
- A company that is involved in adult entertainment.
- A financial institution that derives a part or most of its income from interest (banks, credit unions, etc).

Life Skills 2 Money Management & Employment Skills

WHAT IS HARAM INCOME?

Haram (prohibited) or unlawful income is the income which is not sanctioned by Islam and incurs Allah's displeasure. We have listed some of them earlier. However, it is not limited to a type of product or career, but it includes any income which is earned by lying, cheating or deceiving someone or not working during the work hours without the knowledge of the employer and getting paid for it.

THE EFFECT OF HARAM INCOME ON US

The effect of *haram* income in our lives is drastic and as mentioned earlier, it is a cause for our *du'aas* not being answered. Sometimes tragic and devastating things may happen and we may not realize that our unlawful income may have had a direct impact on us. Additionally, *haram* income will not only affect our **dunya** (this world), but it will also impact our entrance to **Jannah** (paradise). The Prophet *sallAllahu 'alayhi wa sallam* said,

"Nobody which has been nourished with what is unlawful will enter paradise." 77

4 DON'T GET DISTRACTED

We must also remember that the work we do should never take us away from our purpose of life, which is to worship Allah. Allah tells us,

وَمَا خَلَقْتُ ٱلْجِنَّ وَٱلْإِنسَ إِلَّا لِيَعْبُدُونِ

> AND I DID NOT CREATE THE JINN AND MANKIND EXCEPT TO WORSHIP ME. 78

Surah Adh-Dhariyat

And in another *ayah* Allah reminds us that whatever work we do, we must not let it distract us from our share in the Hereafter. Allah tells us,

وَٱبْتَغِ فِيمَآ ءَاتَىٰكَ ٱللَّهُ ٱلدَّارَ ٱلْءَاخِرَةَ ۖ وَلَا تَنسَ نَصِيبَكَ مِنَ ٱلدُّنْيَا

"But seek, through that which Allah has given you, the home of the Hereafter; and [yet], do not forget your share of the world." 79

---

77. Al-Bayhaqi
78. Surah Adh-Dhariyaat [51:56]
79. Surah Al-Qasas [28:77]

HOW SHOULD I CHOOSE MY CAREER?

As discussed earlier, when choosing a career, it is essential that you choose a career path that will not only benefit you in this world but also in the Hereafter. You should choose a career that:

1. Utilizes your passion and skills and will benefit the Muslims as well.

2. Is involved in *halal* activities only.

As you walk down the career path, remember, your career should be one that would help you come closer to Allah. As discussed earlier, the main purpose of all our actions in life is to worship Allah and strive for the Hereafter. Some people get so involved in their careers that they don't have time to pray, fast, read Qur'an or even reflect on their life. This happens when people forget about the main purpose of life and get completely consumed by their careers. Keeping our main purpose of life in focus keeps us grounded and helps us develop balance in our life so we can be successful in this life as well as in the Hereafter.

Your Career as an Act of Worship

Did you know that your day to day deeds can be counted as acts of worship, that is if your intention is to please Allah? You could be eating, drinking, sleeping, studying, or working, and all of this could count for you as good deeds on the Day of Judgement provided that you make an intention to do the act for the sake of Allah.

Muadh ibn Jabal [80] *radhiAllahu 'anhu* once said,

"But I sleep and then get up. I sleep and hope for Allah's reward for my sleep as I seek His reward for my night prayer." [81] We understand from the previous *hadith* that If you sleep with the intention of gaining strength to worship Allah, then your sleep can be counted as an act of worship. If you eat or drink, not just to enjoy your favorite food, but to gain energy to do good deeds, to volunteer at the masjid, recite Qur'an, or pray in the middle of the night, then your eating and drinking can be counted as an act of worship as well. Similarly, your academic and professional career can be counted as an act of worship. The Prophet *sallAllahu 'alayhi wa sallam* taught us,

"When someone spends on his family seeking his reward for it from Allah, it is counted as a *sadaqah* from him." [82]

Therefore, if you study and get a job so you can spend on your family, seeking the reward from Allah, then this counts as *sadaqah* for you. Imagine being rewarded by Allah for studying computer science, biology, or journalism. It can happen, as long as your intention is to worship Allah. When you become this thoughtful and deliberate in every action you do, then you are personifying what Allah tells us in the Qur'an,

قُلْ إِنَّ صَلَاتِي وَنُسُكِي وَمَحْيَايَ وَمَمَاتِي لِلَّهِ رَبِّ الْعَالَمِينَ

"Say, "Indeed, my prayer, my rites of sacrifice, my living and my dying are for Allah, Lord of the worlds." [83]

---

80. Famous and knowledgeable companion of the Prophet *sallAlllahu 'alayhi wa sallam* .
81. Sahih Al-Bukhari
82. Sahih Al-Bukhari and Sahih Muslim
83. Surah Al-An'aam [6:162]

ACTIVITY

What do you notice about these three brothers, their efforts, and their mindsets?

Abdullah

is very career-oriented. He went to the best of schools, got a Bachelor's degree and then a Masters degree. He has a goal to become a millionaire by the age of 30. He is willing to do whatever it takes to achieve that goal. He moves from place to place, switching jobs after jobs, to get a higher pay. He focuses on the financial industry and finally lands a job at a bank as a senior manager. He can see his pathway to becoming an executive at a bank and works hard at it.

Abdullah's brother,

Hassan

has heard from his parents, relatives, and friends that getting a good job in a "hot" field is important. He completes his degree in Computer Science, gets a decent paying job, and is doing well. If he gets a better offer from another employer in another state, he will accept it. He goes to the Masjid to offer his prayers whenever he can, invests a good portion of his earnings, and donates to some charities from time to time. He is overall a nice person.

Life Skills 2 Money Management & Employment Skills

Akram

the youngest of the three brothers, is in high school. He has also heard the same thing that his brothers heard from family, relatives, and friends about the importance of having a good career. But Akram thinks a little differently. He has a burning desire to do something impactful that will leave a legacy for him and that he can benefit from on the Day of Judgment. Everyone works, gets a job, gets married, has kids - but Akram often wonders if that should be the sole purpose of life. He sees that the Muslim community is really entrenched in the western way of banking and financing. His heart aches when he sees all his relatives and friends involved in interest-bearing mortgages, credit card debts, and student loans. He decides that he wants to major in finance so he can learn the financial system well and then work on establishing a *halal* alternative. He faces criticism from everyone around him, but he perseveres and forges ahead so he can do something impactful.

CHAPTER 9

WORKING AS A MUSLIM

Islam encourages etiquette and good conduct in every situation. The importance and effect of making a deeper connection with Allah is seen at the place where we spend the largest part of our time - at work. When we work hard to purify our soul and draw closer to Allah it transforms our character and makes us a positive person. It helps us be more patient, trustworthy and calmer individuals. All these qualities are badly needed in the work environment.

In various surveys, one of the top qualities that employers are seeking in an employee is a positive attitude. A positive attitude benefits both employee and employer. It leads to contentment and productivity at work.

A PERSON WITH A POSITIVE ATTITUDE WILL...

... be open to new ideas and new ways of doing things.

... not feel entitled. The world does not owe them anything. There is humility and humbleness in their demeanor.

... not be a complainer complaining about people and situations.

... ignore workplace gossip.

... understand that hard work is required to earn the respect of peers and supervisors.

... own up to their mistakes and not blame others.

MUSLIM WORKPLACE ETHICS

As Muslims, our work ethic should be distinguished; where we are fully conscious in making sure that every amount of money we earn is *halal*. In our workplace, we must be respectful to people who do not share the same beliefs and values as us. Being professional in our interactions with our supervisors, employees and co-workers, having a positive attitude, working hard and being a good example are the best ways of sharing the true message of Islam and gaining Allah's pleasure. It demonstrates Islam in action and its transformative effect on an individual. Allah tells us,

وَأَحْسِنُوٓاْ إِنَّ ٱللَّهَ يُحِبُّ ٱلْمُحْسِنِينَ

> ... AND DO GOOD; INDEED, ALLAH LOVES THE DOER OF GOOD [84]
>
> **Surah Al-Baqarah**

Our work requires a contract between us and the employer or between us and our staff. If we perform our work with integrity, honesty, diligence and with Muslim work ethics we are fulfilling our obligations as Allah has asked us to do,

"O you who believe! Fulfill (your) obligations" [85]

---

84. Surah Al-Baqarah [2:195]
85. Surah Al-Ma'idah [5:1]

AT WORK

- Bring a *positive* attitude to work
- Always be *punctual* for work
- Work hard & strive for *excellence*
- *Care* and *maintain* all property at the workplace
- Avoid spending time doing *personal* things during working hours
- Always work hard to *complete deadlines*
- When in meetings or during work calls, avoid being on your phone or being *distracted* by other things
- Be *polite* and *respectful* when you are speaking to other coworkers
- Be *patient*
- Always be *honest* and do not clock out late if you are done with work early
- Be *open minded* and *listen* to other people's perspectives
- Avoid *arguments* with coworkers
- *listen* actively and *wait* for your turn to speak

Life Skills 2 Money Management & Employment Skills

Below are a list of some issues at work that Muslims often face and suggestions on how you may handle them.

PRAYING AT WORK

The Prophet sallAllahu 'alayhi wa sallam told us,

"The first action for which a servant of Allah will be held accountable on the Day of Resurrection will be his prayers. If they are in order, he will have prospered and succeeded. If they are lacking, he will have failed and lost. If there is something defective in his obligatory prayers, then the Almighty Lord will say: See if My servant has any voluntary prayers that can complete what is insufficient in his obligatory prayers. The rest of his deeds will be judged the same way." [86]

Your working hard at work should not be at the cost of sacrificing your *salaah*. We need Allah's help in every moment of our lives. If we lose our connection with Allah we invite all sorts of problems to enter our life. It is very important to give Allah the top most priority in your life. Which means that you need to offer your *salaah* at work regardless of your busy schedule. Whenever you start a new job, you should inform those in charge that you need a certain amount of time to pray on time. Praying on time is extremely important as Allah tells us,

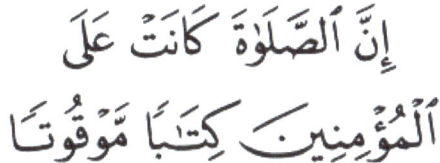

"Indeed, performing prayers is a duty on the believers at the appointed times." [87]

Some Muslims in the west feel shy to pray at their workplace. They feel that making *wudhu* in a public bathroom, or prostrating on the ground in **sajdah** (prostration) in front of people, are all awkward situations. They intentionally miss their prayers at work and then make up missed prayers at home. This is not permissible because *salaah* must be prayed at its proper time. It is important for us to remember that our work is scheduled around our *salaah* and not our *salaah* around our work.

---

86. At-Tirmidhi
87. Surah An-Nisaa [4:103]

TIPS FOR SALAAH AT WORK

- Ask before you start work if you would be allowed to pray at the time of the prayer. Brothers should make sure their employer allows them to take off for **Salaat ul-Jumu'ah**, which is obligatory for brothers to pray in congregation.

- Once you start your job, figure out a quiet and secluded but safe place in the workplace where you can pray at the proper times. You should pray even if you cannot find such a place, but it is a good idea to identify those places ahead of time.

- Figure out a bathroom where you can easily make *wudhu* without attracting too much attention.

- Educate your colleagues in a polite and gentle manner about the requirement of prayer.

- Learn and discuss some of the beneficial effects of prayer on an individual.

- If you usually have meetings around the time of prayer, inform your colleagues and supervisors, and block those times on your calendar so meetings won't be scheduled during those times.

BRAIN TEASER — What are some ways that help you pray on time anywhere?

RESPECTFUL INTERACTION WITH THE OPPOSITE GENDER

In Islam, interactions between the opposite genders are permitted within the boundaries specified in the Qur'an and the *Sunnah*. For many, the boundaries may seem extreme, but there is divine wisdom in it. Of them is to reduce the emotional and social misunderstandings and presumptions which may come about when free mixing occurs at work and other social settings. In most work environments you will inevitably have to interact with the opposite gender. Whether it is during work meetings, professional development sessions, conferences, or work related meals, you will be interacting with them on an ongoing basis. Below are a few helpful guidelines that you should keep in mind as you come across these situations.

1 LOWERING YOUR GAZE

Have you ever felt uncomfortable when someone is staring at you? It is more uncomfortable when someone from the opposite gender does so. To protect our dignity and honor Allah has asked us to lower our gaze and to look away instead of staring at each other's face or eyes upon seeing, meeting or talking to each other. While in some cultures, it is considered a sign of dishonesty to look away while talking or a sign of being overly shy, these are no doubt only perceptions which change over time. Allah has created us, He alone knows what works best for us. Allah tells us in the Qur'an, addressing both men and women separately,

قُل لِّلْمُؤْمِنِينَ يَغُضُّوا۟ مِنْ أَبْصَـٰرِهِمْ وَيَحْفَظُوا۟ فُرُوجَهُمْ

"Tell the believing men to reduce [some] of their vision and guard their private parts..." [88]

---

88. Surah An-Nur [24:30]

Life Skills 2 Money Management & Employment Skills | 89

وَقُل لِّلْمُؤْمِنَٰتِ يَغْضُضْنَ مِنْ أَبْصَٰرِهِنَّ وَيَحْفَظْنَ فُرُوجَهُنَّ

"And tell the believing women to reduce [some] of their vision and guard their private parts..." 89

2   SHAKING HANDS

It is customary for people in the workplace to shake hands as it is considered a professional and polite way of greeting one another. Whereas not shaking hands is often considered impolite and rude. Even in Islam we are commanded to greet each other with a handshake. It was mentioned in a *hadith* that a man said, *"O Messenger of Allah, when a man among us meets his brother or friend, should he bow for him?"* The Prophet, peace and blessings be upon him, said, *"No."* The man said, *"Should he embrace him and kiss him?"* The Prophet said, *"No."* The man said, *"Should he shake his hand?"* The Prophet said, *"Yes."* 90

However, we know from the Prophet *sallAllahu 'alayhi wa sallam's* actions that He *sallAllahu 'alayhi wa sallam* did not shake hands with the opposite gender. As Islam is a complete way of life, our Prophet *sallAllahu 'alayhi wa sallam* showed us how to maintain cross gender respect for each other without physical touch. His wife Aisha *radhiAllahu 'anha* said,

"By Allah, the hand of the Messenger of Allah *sallAllahu 'alayhi wa sallam* never touched the hand of any woman. 91 He would take the oath of allegiance from them verbally." 92

The Prophet *sallAllahu 'alayhi wa sallam* respected women greatly and would go out of his way to help and fulfill their needs. However, he showed us that women and men can still respect and honor each other without any need of physical contact. He told us, "I do not shake hands with women." 93

In light of the above mentioned *hadith* and from the example of the Prophet *sallAllahu 'alayhi wa sallam*, it is impermissible for a man to shake a woman's hand, or for a woman to shake a man's hand who is *not his or her* **mahram**. 94 Oftentimes, not knowing or understanding the Islamic

---

89. Surah An-Nur [24:31]
90. At-Tirmidhi
91. "Any woman" here is referring to a woman who is not his mother, daughter, wife, aunt or niece.
92. Sahih Muslim
93. Ibn Majah
94. *Mahram*, in Islam is a term referred to a husband, wife or a family member with whom marriage is not allowed. (For example, a woman's *mahram* is her father, son, brother, uncle, nephew).

Life Skills 2 Money Management & Employment Skills

stance on gender relations, Muslims find themselves ignoring or compromising Islamic principles in these situations in favor of not being considered rude or impolite. However, people in general tend to be very respectful of religious observances of other religions. When explained in a respectful way the reason for not shaking hands is generally a sharing moment of your faith and its beauty and it is usually much appreciated.

HANDSHAKING AT WORK

When you are meeting a business client, a co-worker or anyone who happens to be of the opposite gender, they will most likely want to shake hands with you since it is considered customary and professional.

Remember, every situation can be an opportunity for you to educate others about Islam and share this beautiful way of life. Most people will appreciate your effort and time to educate them.

To help avoid an uneasy situation, here are some suggestions:

- Write a polite email explaining your hand shaking preferences
- Talk to your supervisor and/or to the person before a meeting
- Invite a speaker to inform your place of work about Islamic values and custom
- Do a presentation about Islamic customs and etiquettes for your co-workers

When you give precedence to Allah by applying an Allah-centric approach to daily life situations and put your trust in Him, He will always make your situations easy. As He tells us,

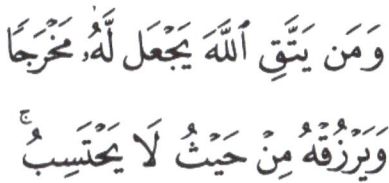

"...And whoever fears Allah – He will make for him a way out. And will provide for him from where he does not expect..." [95]

---

95. Surah At-Talaaq [65:2-3]

Life Skills 2 Money Management & Employment Skills | 91

4 COMMON EMPLOYMENT BENEFITS

Employment benefits are forms of perks or compensation that are provided to employees in addition to their salaries. Many companies offer a wide range of benefits as part of their contract, before accepting any benefits always make sure that it is permissible in Islam. As long as there is nothing prohibited about a specific benefit, and that a specific benefit is not abused, there should not be any issue in taking them. Here are some benefits that companies offer and a brief summary of the rulings on these benefits:

1. PERSONAL/ SICK DAYS

These are a certain number of days included in a company's contract that employees can take off if they are sick or for any other personal reasons. There is nothing wrong with taking these days off since they are agreed upon in the contract. However, sometimes people "call out sick" when they are not really sick (for example, go on a leisure trip, or take advantage of a good sale) and that is considered a lie, which is a sin in Islam.

2. PUBLIC HOLIDAYS:

Your employment benefit package will have public holidays off. If you work at a hospital or any service related field where workers are working round the clock even on public holidays then you can use that opportunity to arrange with your supervisor to work on a public holiday and take off on important Muslim holidays.

3. RETIREMENT PLANS

Some companies offer retirement plans where they put aside a certain amount of money for the employee. Sometimes companies encourage employees to invest for their retirement also by matching whatever the employee puts aside. This money is then invested in some companies, mutual funds, and sometimes in fixed-income securities (like bonds). If the money is invested in a company that deals with prohibited products and services, or it is invested in a fixed-income security, then it is not permissible to take the profit from those investments. A Muslim employee should strive to have that money invested in a *halal* investment. If he/she is not allowed to choose the investments, then the profits resulting from the investments should not be accepted.

4. INSURANCE

Insurance as is offered today is generally not allowed in Islam. However, scholars have cited exceptions where it is absolutely necessary, such as; health, car, house, workman compensation and disability insurance. In these instances it is permissible to have insurance. As well as life insurance which is offered to you as part of your benefit package from your work is allowed. However, buying your own life insurance is not permitted in Islam.

UNIT 2

REVIEW AND REFLECT QUESTIONS

1

Abdullah is too embarrassed to pray at work so he joins his *dhuhr* and ʻ*asr* prayers together. Is this permissible for him to do?

2

Why is it important to inform a potential employer about your Islamic beliefs when getting a new job?

3

List three ways to help you be punctual for work.

4

Anisa and her best friend Manal have been planning for years to start an online Hijab business together. Anisa and Manal are very close and have regular meetings about their ideas and how much each will get paid. At one of the meetings Manal told Anisa that she didn't keep her word about how they each would get paid. Anisa got mad at Manal and said, "I don't remember ever saying that." Name some things they should have done that could have helped avoid such a conflict?

APPENDIX

EXPLANATION OF SCENARIOS IN CHAPTER 8

1

Abdullah, who was working in a bank. The bank is a place which usually derives much of its income from interest. By working there, Abdullah is supporting and promoting those interest-bearing transactions, which is a form of cooperation in sin and aggression. Abdullah should do whatever he can to come out of this job and try to find a job in a place where he is not promoting things that are displeasing to Allah. Abdullah should feel reassured that if he leaves this job then Allah will replace it with something better for him. The Prophet *sallAllahu 'alayhi wa sallam* said, "*Verily, you will never leave anything for the sake of Allah Almighty but that Allah will replace it with something better for you.*" [96]

2

Hassan, did he have a purposeful career? Not really. Hassan followed the stereotype of what the society told him to do: Earn a degree, get a good job, enjoy life, and from time to time, donate something to the Masjid if you can. Though there may not be something inherently haram about what Hassan was doing, it is certainly not in full alignment with the greater purpose of our life, which is to worship Allah.

3

Looking at Akram's situation, you notice that his academic and professional career choices were grounded in wanting to serve Allah, establishing His way, and offering a unique and needed service to the Muslims. Earning money was important and was not ignored, but was not the primary focus of his career. He wanted to utilize his intellect and the talents Allah has given him to seek the Hereafter yet at the same time he did not ignore his portion of the world. Thus, Akram's career was more purposeful.

---

96. Ahmad

EXCERPT FROM AMJA's[97] RULING ON COLLEGE LOANS

THE RULING CONCERNING STUDENT LOANS

Before giving a ruling for such loans, one must have a complete conception of the need for these loans in general and the need for them by Muslim students in the United States in particular. The following premises must be understood:

First, university education is of great concern to hundreds of thousands of Muslims in the United States. Those who live in this country are greatly in need of higher education. Thus, this need falls under a "general need," to say the least, as understood in *fiqh*.

Second, university study in the United States is very expensive and is increasing faster than the rate of inflation. In fact, 50% of those qualified to enter college did not attend college due to financial costs.

Third, numerous sources of financial assistance are available to students in general. Some grants, for example, can cover about 50% of student fees. Fourth, over 60% of university students have student loans. These are not only full-time students, but this number includes over 50% of those students who have jobs as well.

At the same time, though, borrowing in the United States is not always due to "need" as defined in a *fiqh* sense. Borrowing and paying for things over time is part of the American culture—of which Muslims are

---

97. American Muslim Jurists of America is an organizations of Muslim scholars.

part. So those who are not in need as well as those in need both borrow and pay interest. Even the level for "financial need" does not mean that the person is in a state of "need" from a *fiqh* perspective, as the federal standard for that is much different than the standard for begging in Islam or receiving *zakat*. Furthermore, when people apply for financial aid, it is typical that they do not actually state all of their income. Hence, it looks like they are in need while, in reality, they are not.

THE RULING

Given the above premises, the following conclusions can be made:

▶ FIRST

A subsidized governmental loan in which the interest payments are covered by the government means that such a loan is not a *ribawi* (interest-bearing) loan from the outset, as the government who gave the loan pays the interest as well.

▶ SECOND

Interest does enter into this subsidized loan through other means. The student agrees to pay the interest on the loan if he does not pay off the entire principle six months after his graduation. In this case, the loan would not be considered forbidden on its own merit-or intends what is forbidden-as it is possible for the student to pay off the entire loan without any interest during those six months. Thus, the prohibitive aspect is that it is a means to what is forbidden and not that it is forbidden in and of itself.

▶ THIRD

"The act that is prohibited on its own merit is permissible only in case of necessity while that which is prohibited only as a means to something prohibited is permissible in case of need or overwhelming benefit."[98] Based on this principle, education is a need, as we have shown. Therefore, it is permissible for a Muslim student to receive a subsidized loan if he believes that he will be able to repay all of it during the specific period, if he has a true need for such a loan. He would be in need if neither he nor his parents have the money to pay for his education and he is not able to get a scholarship or grant to cover his costs. Additonally, he is not able to earn enough money through work to pay for his schooling. In such a case, he can take a loan to meet his needs only, as what is done on the basis of need has to be restricted to what is needed only.

---

98. Al-Qaraafi, al-Furooq (Dar-us-salaam, 2008), P.58.

▶ FOURTH

As for unsubsidized loans, their impermissibility is clear as they contain interest. So they are haram based on their own merit and can only be permissible in a state of necessity. So it is not permissible for a Muslim to resort to them as university education is not considered a necessity according to the majority of contemporary scholars.

▶ FIFTH

The following points need further investigation:

A At what point could university education be considered a necessity allowing interest bearing loans.

B Could the maxim, "a general need is to be treated like a necessity for permitting forbidden acts" be invoked for student loans due to the general need for them.

C Could there be a difference between starting education with a student loan as opposed to resorting to a student loan to continue one's education, based on the maxim, "What occurs to continue something could be overlooked while it would not be overlooked when beginning it."

D If such loans are considered permissible, would they extend to all levels or education or simply the minimum needed.

This is an important issue to discuss because the cost of a college education is increasing and the need for a college education is something agreed upon by all intelligent people. Therefore, one must ask: What is the default ruling concerning student loans? What is the ruling if there is no viable alternative to a student loan for a person's education? If it is permissible, is it permissible in order to obtain a higher degree or one must discontinue such loans after completing the degree that one absolutely needs?

For detailed ruling regarding college loans please visit amjaonline.org

FREQUENTLY USED EXPRESSIONS

1 *Subhaanahu wa ta'aala*: May He (Allah) be Glorified and Exalted.

This expression is used in combination with Allah's name or when referring to Him.

2 *SallAllahu 'alayhi wa sallam*: May Allah's peace and blessings be upon him.

This is the *du'aa* that Allah has asked us to make whenever the name of the Prophet Muhammad *sallAllahu 'alayhi wa sallam* is mentioned. Allah commands us,

'Indeed, Allah confers blessing upon the Prophet, and His angels (ask Him to do so). O you who have believed, ask (Allah to confer) blessing upon him and ask (Allah to grant him) peace."[99]

The Prophet *sallAllahu 'alayhi wa sallam* also told us,

"The one who offers salah for me from my Ummah, sincerely from their heart, Allah will then offer ten salahs for them, will raise them ten degrees, write for them ten good deeds, and cancel for them ten sins."[100]

'Alayhis salaam: May Allah's peace be on him.

3 This expression is a *du'aa* which is used whenever referring to a Prophet of Allah other than Prophet Muhammad *sallAllahu 'alayhi wa sallam*.

RadhiAllahu 'anhu: May Allah be pleased with him.

4 This expression is a *du'aa* which is usually used whenever referring to a companion of the Prophet Muhammad *sallAllahu 'alayhi wa sallam*.

---

99. Surah Al-Ahzab [33:56]
100. An-Nasa'ee

MONTHLY BUDGET Planner

ITEMS	AMOUNT	NOTES
DIVIDE THE BI-WEEKLY AMOUNT BY THREE		
EXPENSES		
TAXES		
CAR		
RENT		
WATER		
GAS		
ELECTRICITY		
INTERNET		
PHONE		
GROCERIES		
CLOTHING		
SADAQAH		
FAMILY MEMBERS		
CLOSE RELATIVES		
MASJID		
ISLAMIC SCHOOL		
ORPHANS		
GIFTS		
LOANS		
INVESTMENTS		
PRECIOUS METALS		
MUTUAL FUNDS / STOCKS		
OTHER		
TOTAL		

CHECK OUT OUR OTHER BOOKS!

NOW AVAILABLE AT AMAZON

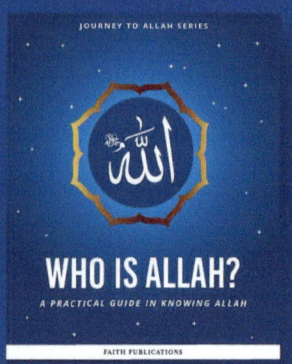
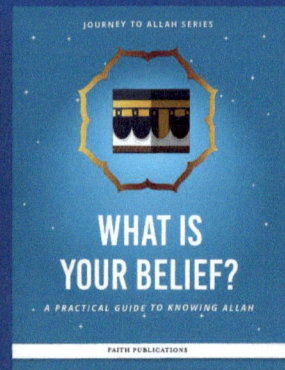
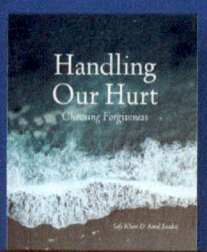

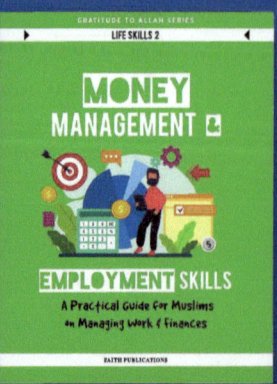

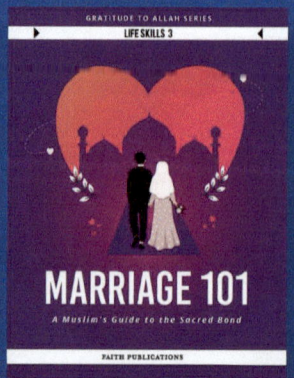

FAITH Publications

www.ingramcontent.com/pod-product-compliance
Lightning Source LLC
Chambersburg PA
CBHW041545220426
43665CB00002B/39